Portable Roots

Portable Roots:
Transplanting the Bicultural Child

By

Jeanne Stevenson-Moessner

Portable Roots: Transplanting the Bicultural Child
By Jeanne Stevenson-Moessner

This book first published 2014

Cambridge Scholars Publishing

12 Back Chapman Street, Newcastle upon Tyne, NE6 2XX, UK

British Library Cataloguing in Publication Data
A catalogue record for this book is available from the British Library

ISBN (10): 1-4438-5697-5, ISBN (13): 978-1-4438-5697-3

To my students at The Black Forest Academy in Kandern, Germany,

Who first taught me about portable roots,

To the former inhabitants of the Basel Mission's Children's Home,

Who tutored me in their tenacity and courage,

To the wise men and women of Princeton, New Jersey,

Who mentored me by their lives of resilience!

TABLE OF CONTENTS

LIST OF ILLUSTRATIONS

LIST OF COLOUR PLATES

See Colour Centrefold

FOREWORD

LIVING ON A BRIDGE

We are blessed and cursed for the fact that we live on a bridge. I will never be totally American, never totally African. When insecure, which is more common, I don't belong anywhere....I share [my parents'] commitment now, but I still have no roots. (Edgar, the adult son of Protestant missionaries, serving in Ghana)

As a researcher, I find myself on two bridges – one is theological and one is personal. Theologically, on one side of the bridge, the prevailing view in mainstream theological circles is that of post-colonialism which includes a critique of the assumption that one culture has the right to evangelize within another.[1] Reflecting on missions in the 19th, 20th, and 21st centuries in particular, theologians question the movement of European or North American missionaries into regions underdeveloped in their economies, medical systems, educational opportunities, and Christian exposure. This discourse often assumes that all missionaries were enacting an imperialistic mindset. On the other side of the bridge, there is lack of interest in exploring the possible connections between forms of colonialism and mission.

In this theological debate, many children have been swept under the bridge of discussion.[2] The children and adolescents who comprised my

---

[1] One comprehensive and controversial study, *Re-Thinking Missions: A Laymen's Inquiry After One Hundred Years*, By the Commission of Appraisal, was spearheaded by William Ernest Hocking, funded by John D. Rockefeller, (New York: Harper & Row, 1932). One reaction to the study, John Fitzmier and Randall Balmer's "A Poultice for the Bite of the Cobra: The Hocking Report and the Presbyterian Missions in the Middle Decades of the Twentieth Century," in *The Diversity of Discipleship: Presbyterians and Twentieth-Century Christian Witness,* eds. Milton Coalter, John Mulder, Louis Weeks (Louisville: Westminster/John Knox, 1991) actually brings the issues into more recent debate.

[2] There is mention of problems in education of the missionary's children in such works as *Rethinking Missions: A Laymen's Inquiry After One Hundred Years*, ibid., p.297. Hocking mentioned the serious problems of the establishment of special schools, the expenses of tuition and travel, the long separations "at a time when children are going through difficult periods of adjustment to different modes of

earliest research samples were missionary dependents. Their lives were often shaped by their parents' well-intentioned vocational decisions. In the theological assessments of mission strategy, ideologies, and sending agencies, debaters, defenders, and critics inadvertently allow the dependents [the bicultural children] who were/are relatively powerless in the past mission endeavors to be caught in the undertow of inquiry.

I have read a few accounts of privilege[3] yet scores of narratives with tales of sacrifice, deprivation, altruism, and loyalty among missionaries serving nationals. In various wars, missionaries were imprisoned or killed. Medical missionaries created hospitals, started tuberculosis clinics, acquired pharmaceuticals from their home countries, and helped care for the poor, the leprous, and the dying. Education missionaries addressed illiteracy and further helped nationals to go on for higher education in Britain, Canada, and the USA. Some of those nationals chose to stay in these countries and even today are leading researchers, academics, and business professionals.

In the 19th and early 20th centuries, young children of British, Canadian, and USA missionaries often died from cholera, diphtheria, and tuberculosis. Pearl Buck, for example, lost four siblings, all buried in China: Maude died from starvation; Edith died from cholera; Arthur died of a fever; and Clyde died of diphtheria. Pearl's older brother, Edwin, struggled with dysentery but survived it. That left, out of seven children, Edwin, Pearl, and Comfort.

The Basel Mission in Basel, Switzerland, sought to circumvent this risk of infant mortality by requiring their missionaries to leave their young children in the Basel Children's Home (*das Kinderhaus*) until it closed in 1948. I interviewed 39 of these adult children. If their parents went to Africa [Ghana, Cameroon, Nigeria, or Sudan], the separation was 3 years; if India, five years; if China, 8 years. Some of the Swiss and German missionaries to China did not make it back in World War II. The call to missions came with a cost. Let us not forget the children whose lives were shaped by this call.

I also stand on a bridge between the "objects of my research" [missionary children] and my own self as subject. By "objects of research," I do not mean the interviewees are objectified. Rather, they are the topics – as living human documents. Their lives are the raw data of discovery! The bridge on which I stand is perhaps the inter-subjectivity

---

living, to different countries, and to different peoples." Hocking concluded there had been no adequate solution to the problem.

[3] For example, Stanley Elwood Brush, *Farewell The Winterline: Memories of a Boyhood in India* (Santa Rosa: Chipkali, 2002).

between subject and object. Empirical research according to astrophysicist Piet Hut needs to name this interaction between subject and "object."[4] In addition to standard questions, compilation of data and responses, recorded interviews, tables, and charts, what else is imbedded in the conscious experience of me, the researcher as subject?

In 1978, I was a schoolteacher in an international school in Europe, a school that was populated largely by children of missionaries from Canada and the USA. I heard the children express their cultural dislocation or dissolution, often in terms of *rootlessness*. The school was neither European, nor North American, rather a hybrid of the two. Dr. James Loder of Princeton Theological Seminary and I discussed the cultural dynamics of these children of missionaries. These children were often separated from their parents, lived in dormitories, and were raised by surrogate parents (dorm parents). Why would I feel so drawn to them? Then, my location on yet another bridge became clear. I had also been raised by a surrogate mother.

The next pages contain true stories of children who lived "on a bridge." At times, the bridge spanned two hemispheres, two continents, two cultures, or two homes. In some cases, the bridge itself was home. I close with a poem from someone living on a bridge spanning North America and Asia:

Imli, neem, kayla, ahm;
Sitaphal, guava, papaya, palm;
Rhododendron, white oak, deodar;
Acacia, coconut, gul mohar;
Catalpa, frangipani, cashew, lime;
Walnut, redbud, spruce, elm, and pine;
Maples on fire, flame of the forest:
Two hemispheres – one chorus.[5]

Imli, Neem, Kayla, Ahm
Verda Hostetler Bialac, Woodstock School, India, 1955

---

[4] Piet Hut, "The Evolving Empirical Method of Science," The 2012 William Witherspoon Lecture in Theology and the Natural Sciences, March 23, 2012, Princeton, NJ, Center of Theological Inquiry.
[5] *Living on the Edge: Tales of Woodstock School*, eds. Sally Stoddard, Charlene Connell, Catherine Hinz, Sally Woolever (Mukilteo, WA: Kodai Woodstock International, 2004), p.275.

ACKNOWLEDGEMENTS

When my husband and I were doctoral students at The University of Basel, Switzerland, we often took inexpensive student flights through Reykjavik, Iceland, to get back to the States. These flights seemed so precarious that I used to give the earlier manuscript for this book to a colleague in the event our plane did not reach its destination. I would tell her: "If anything happens to me, make sure it gets published!" This book is my most important work because it contains the narratives of so many courageous people.

First, I must give credit to the vivacious students at The Black Forest Academy in Kandern, Germany. I was newly married to David Moessner and newly-minted from my first teaching position at St. Mary's Episcopal School in Memphis, Tennessee. St.Mary's remains one of the most progressive, well-endowed schools of excellence in the southeastern part of the United States. My difficulty there was in choosing which piece of technology to use in a classroom. Within a few months of my marriage in 1975, I was teaching at the Black Forest Academy where the only piece of equipment (on loan from Ramstein Military Base) was a movie projector with reels! Movies were greatly appreciated in my classes, especially the one on sex education for which I almost lost my job. Needless to say, the rapid contrast in the two settings created a learning curve for me.

Everything I had learned as first a student and later a teacher at St.Mary's Episcopal School was needed. The mentors I had had in Mary Davis, Nat Hughes, Katherine Phillips, Fanny Ware, Mrs. Gilmore Lynn, Presh Baker Gill, and Andy Banks taught me that the classroom is a sacred place of trust. They showed me that a child can learn better in a safe and compassionate environment. Trust, safety, compassion, and mutual respect translated into the Black Forest Academy with its minimum of accouterments.

The students respected me as I respected them, and we learned together. Occasionally, I got a shock as when Jeff Bettig fell out the back window into a vegetable patch. Most often, I was humbled by the gratefulness of the children. This school was founded by the Janz Team of Canada predominantly for children of missionaries although the school attracted children of diplomats, business people, and native Germans. The textbooks were very used books that were no longer in use in the Canadian

Saskatchewan school system. When I taught, I looked at the words written on the spines: REJECT. After some months, I contacted the Women of the Church (Second Presbyterian) in Memphis, Tennessee. In due time, a couple of large boxes arrived in that small village of Germany, boxes from Houghlin Mifflin Co. I watched the ninth graders open those boxes in class. For many of them, it was the first time they ever had a brand new, glossy textbook. To this day, I remember how they sniffed the fresh scent of newness and handled the books like newborns.

It is to them that I dedicate this book. They first articulated to me a sense of "homelessness" or "rootlessness" geographically. They trusted me with their stories and took lengthy questionnaires for my research. Thank you.

The University of Basel invested in my research by awarding me the Karl Barth Stipendium. With the money, I travelled by train and bus all through southern Germany to interview thirty-nine- former inhabitants of the Basel Mission, (*das Kinderhaus der Basler Mission*). These people did not know me, but they all opened their homes and hearths to me. They gave me something to eat and drink; they shared photos and memorabilia with me. They walked me to the train station. They cared for me as I hope to care for their stories. To my dear friends of the Basel Mission, I pray I have been faithful to what you invested in me. I dedicate this book to you.

All the while, a "miscellaneous sample" for my research was growing. This sample contained some seasoned adults who reside in the Princeton, New Jersey, environs. Thanks to an invitation from Princeton's Center of Theological Inquiry, a grant from the University Research Council of Southern Methodist University, and letters of reference from Robin Lovin, Ruben Habito, Elsie McKee, and Shannon Jung – I was able to spend a research leave interviewing these remarkable adults who had come to terms with their "portable roots."

Now I am at peace with the length of time it has taken to see this book into print. I needed to grow with the material. Thank you to my editors at Cambridge Scholars Publishing who believed in this work: Sean Howley, Adam Terry, Keith Thaxton, and Carol Koulikourdi. There were also individuals along the way who were positioned to help me: the late David Laird Dungan, Peter and Jennifer Jenkins, Rev. Dr. Ruth Epting, Dr. Stephanie Klein, Dean James Quick, the late Loulou Cullmann, Blanche Butler Montesi, Karen Lull, Holly Newman, Dr. Roberta Berger, Frau Hannah Brodbeck, Carolyn Douglas, Duane Harbin, Becky Waugh, Mary Davis, Rev. Dr. Susan Sharpe, and Kempie Craddock Jenkins. Jean Moessner prepared the graphics. Deanna Hollas undertook the technical responsibility of preparing this book for print, and she has done it well!

My husband, Dave Moessner, and our two grown children, David and Jean, have always believed in me. Like the Black Forest Academy students smelling their new textbooks, may I never take this for granted!

I speak quite a bit about *resilience* toward the end of the book. During this last phase of the book, one person in particular has modeled resilience in her victory lap with cancer, and that is Kempie Craddock Jenkins. As she has sat in treatment rooms, she has prayed this work into print. Her ability to fathom a larger picture reminds me that this work is more than a compilation of words and sheaves of paper. Thank you, Kempie, for reminding me of the Resilience of God.

Jeanne Stevenson-Moessner
February 18, 2014
Dallas, Texas, USA

CHAPTER ONE

PORTABLE ROOTS

I have learned for so many years to live with my roots packed in soil, and each place that I go, I brush a little of the soil of the place over the roots, but I never unpack them. [It is like they are wrapped in a burlap sack, penetrable to water.] You just brush a little bit of the soil of the place over it so you're as inconspicuous as possible. (Edgar, missionary son, after his return to the USA from Ghana).

Rootedness

Edgar gave the image of "portable roots" that I needed to begin my investigation. For over four years, I had taught school in what is now being described as a hybrid or "third culture" and had heard from students many variations of "rootlessness" or social dislocation. Edgar was the first to articulate so clearly this feeling of nomadic transience. His "portable roots" were like those of saplings in a plant nursery with a burlap sack around them. "You just brush a little bit of the soil of the place over it [roots] so you're as inconspicuous as possible."

Four years earlier, Edgar had described "living on a bridge" between cultures. This experience of being "betwixt and between" has also been expressed by children of military, diplomats, businesspeople, refugees, and immigrants.[1] In Australia, for example, aboriginal children who are now regarded as the "lost generation" or the "stolen generation" are speaking

---

[1] *Unrooted Childhoods: Memoirs of Growing Up Global*, editors Faith Eidse and Nina Sichel, (London: Nicholas Brealey Publishing, 2004). Narratives are from adult children of Foreign Service officers, of professors, of diplomats, of military, of missionaries, of businesspersons. It was not uncommon for the parents to be of two different nationalities. For example, Tara Bahrampour's architect father was Iranian while her singer mother was North American (Californian). Tara has not only grown up in two nations (Iran and USA), but she has watched the two nations at war. See her chapter "To See and See Again," in *Unrooted Childhoods*, p. 199-207.

out in art, film, and literature about their uprootedness.[2] What became significant in the following excerpt is Edgar's introduction of the import of the *religious matrix* for children of missionaries. The faith or religious commitment of the parents not only permeates the missionary community but leads the children to "living on a bridge."

> [Faith] has given our lives their shape. The fact that our parents are committed to it has determined where we are born, where educated, who our friends are, the fact we fit in no culture. We don't. We are blessed and cursed for the fact that we live on a bridge. I will never be totally American, never totally African. When insecure, which is more common, I don't belong anywhere. ...I share [my parents'] commitment now, but I still have no roots.

Not all children of missionaries respond to the *religious matrix* in the same way, of course. These responses will be considered in Chapter Five. What is consistent in all the narratives is the refrain of "life on a bridge." One adult daughter of missionaries to Seoul, Korea, described herself as a cultural traveler stuck on a "tenuous log bridge with the washed out road behind."[3] This slippery bridge becomes a balancing act.[4] After her return to the USA, she did enlist in the Peace Corps and was assigned to South Korea for five years. However, the world of her childhood had changed. Like her parents before her, she relied on faith to carry her forward.[5] When one moves forward, there is then the experience of life in a "double world."

> I grew up in a double world, the small white clean Presbyterian American world of my parents and the big loving merry not-too-clean Chinese world, and there was no communication between them. When I was in the Chinese world I was Chinese, I spoke Chinese and behaved as a Chinese and ate as the Chinese did, and I shared their thoughts and feelings. When I was in the American world, I shut the door between.[6] [Pearl S. Buck]

"Double worlds" exist for those intimate with more than one culture. Such were the "worlds" of bicultural children like the writer and philanthropist Pearl Sydenstricker Buck. Buck, the first American woman

---

[2] *Half Light Portraits From Black Australia* (Sydney: Art Gallery of New South Wales, 2008).

[3] Donna Sidwell DeGracia, *An Intricate Tapestry: The Acculturation of Missionaries and Their Children* (Minneapolis: Kirk House, 2011), p.168.

[4] Ibid., p.64.

[5] Ibid., p.168.

[6] Pearl S. Buck, *My Several Worlds* (New York: John Day Company, 1954), p.10.

to win a Nobel Prize in Literature (1938), had previously received the Pulitzer Prize for *The Good Earth*, a novel which testifies to her intimacy with China. *Cultural intimacy* is deep understanding and close association with a physical place, a region, a country, or a nation. My research is an exploration of the impact of "double or multiple worlds" on the developing child. It includes both the consolidation, union or merger of these worlds as well as the dissolution, fragmentation, or splitting of these worlds.

In 1900, in the springtime of the Yangtse River Valley, Pearl Buck's worlds split apart with the Boxer Uprising (Yihetuan Movement). "I felt my world splitting unexpectedly into its parts...I could not understand why we, who were still ourselves and unchanged, should be lumped with unknown white men from unknown countries who had been what we were not, robbers and plunderers....I was innocent, but because I had the fair skin, the blue eyes, the blond hair of my race I was hated, and because of fear of me and my kind I walked in danger."[7]

Pearl Buck spent most of the first forty years of her life in China (Chinkiang, Shanghai, Nanhsuchou, Nanking). In 1934, because of conditions in China, and to be closer to Richard Walsh and her daughter Carol who was institutionalized in New Jersey, Buck moved permanently to the USA. She became active in American civil rights and women's rights as well as in cultural exchanges between Asia and the West. She and her husband founded Welcome House, the first international, inter-racial adoption agency. For Amerasian children who were considered "unadoptable," Buck established the Pearl S. Buck Foundation to sponsor funding for literally thousands of children in several Asian countries. In such an odyssey, Pearl Buck came to terms with her several worlds. She summarized: "I have never been an evangelical missionary, and indeed abhor the general notion, and yet I know very well that my missionary beginnings have shaped me to the extent of feeling responsible at least for what I can do personally about a given situation which needs mending."[8]

My research assistant, Deanna Hollas, asked me recently if I had known Pearl Buck personally. My frequent mention of Pearl Buck in my research had prompted this understandable question. Her query allowed me to understand and articulate "why" I had utilized the life and narratives of Pearl Buck so often. Buck was able to articulate with her gift of words and her skills in writing her life as a "bicultural." In addition, almost like a pioneer in the field of psycho-social analysis, she was able to explain the consequences and effects of "double or multiple worlds."

---

[7] Ibid., p.33.
[8] Ibid., p.371.

Since the lifetime of Pearl Buck, there has been a groundswell of interest in "rootedness" and the significance of place. Many examples will follow but this sampling will serve as an introduction. In their recent work, *Practicing Care in Rural Congregations and Communities*, authors Shannon Jung, Joretta Marshall, and Jeanne Hoeft make one major claim: physical location, or place, matters to identity, worldview, and way of life.[9] This heightened awareness is particularly acute for those in rural communities. A matter for theological reflection becomes the meaning of "home" and the need of people for a place to belong. "....rootedness is disrupted by the mobility of the postmodern world. The meaning of home and attachment to place might have changed given new virtual realities, but we are nevertheless embodied, emplaced human beings who are always located somewhere."[10] The struggle with rootedness is expressed by novelists such as Jhumpa Lahiri, Indian American author of *The Namesake* and Pulitzer Prize for Fiction winner, who never knows how to answer the question: where are you from? "The question of identity is always a difficult one, but especially so for those who are culturally displaced, as immigrants are, or those who grow up in two worlds simultaneously, as is the case for their children."[11] As the daughter of Bengali immigrants, Ms. Lahiri writes about her feelings of dislocation and rootlessness. "In the U.S., we were rootless, transplanted individuals who had no connection to anybody by blood."[12]

The importance of a child's primary caretakers and the early sensory imprint of "place" are clearly and painfully depicted in the movie "Philomena," based on the true story of Philomena Lee. As an unwed teenager, Philomena was sent to the Sean Ross Abbey in Roscrea, Ireland, where she gave birth to a son, Anthony. As Philomena worked off her debt to the nuns in hard labor, the nuns sold her son for a thousand pounds to an American couple. Philomena searched for her son for fifty years on a journey that took her from Ireland to America. She found that her son had been a successful lawyer in Washington with a devoted partner. Her son died of AIDS some years before her trip to America. Although the Irish nuns thwarted all attempts of Philomena to locate him, although they lied to him that he had "been abandoned" by his mother, Martin chose to be buried in the Abbey's graveyard in Ireland. This is where his mother

---

[9] Shannon Jung, Jeanne Hoeft, Joretta Marshall, *Practicing Care in Rural Congregations and Communities* (Minneapolis: Fortress Press, 2013), p.14.
[10] Ibid., pp.39-40.
[11] Interview with Alexandra Wolfe, "Jhumpa Lahiri: On Dislocation" in Wall Street Journal, September 20, 2013, Life and Culture Section.
[12] Ibid.

eventually "found him," in the place of his birth and earliest human recollection.

The Case of Mike

The elaborate psycho-social excursion of those who spend their childhood and adolescent years in more than one culture is an odyssey. An odyssey is a long journey, filled with challenges, successes, and adventures. Sometimes, the challenge is filled with loss. Mike, son of missionaries, was able to articulate this loss in the interview (below).[13] He, like Pearl Buck, attempted to live in several "worlds" and saw them split apart. At the time of the interview, he did not have the maturity to integrate the cultures as was evidenced by Pearl Buck in her later life.

"So I lost Africa."[14] Mike said this with such sadness that it seemed he had lost part of himself. Mike was the child of two cultures. He was born to Caucasian North American missionaries who founded a small African mission school in Cameroon. Mike attended this school in the late 1970s and grew up through his late adolescence with Africans as his closest friends. He lived in two French-speaking African countries [Cameroon and the Democratic Republic of Congo]. When he was about seventeen, his parents started to tell him: "You've got to start acting like a white man." According to Mike, he had gradually been elevated to the position of elder in the village, even in a culture where age was usually required for such authority. He was expected "to become 'white'" which implied more responsibility and privilege. He was eventually not allowed to eat with his Cameroonian friends. "So I lost Africa. Up to that point, I always thought I would live in Africa the rest of my life…I lost Africa."

His parents sent him to a Bible school in France. There, he chose a French girlfriend. Mike's continuing and understandable attempts to relocate himself from one French-speaking country to another raised the concerns of the North American missionary authorities who decided he was "emotionally unbalanced." He was sent to America. Mike: "Before I could grow emotionally or spiritually, I had to come to terms with my American identity. So I went back to America to satisfy my critics once and for all."

Mike tried to go back to Cameroon alone on business. He was working as a liaison between the mission and the Cameroonian government, and he

---

[13] Jeanne Stevenson-Moessner, "Cultural Dissolution: 'I Lost Africa'" in *Missiology: An International Review*, Vol.XIV, No.3, July 1986, p.313-324.

[14] Note: Africa is comprised of 52 distinct countries. I am retaining Mike's wording to illustrate his "worlds" at the time of the interview.

had quite a large salary. "Well to make a long story short, I became malnourished because of the guilt I had of being able to feed myself when kids I had known as a child were going hungry. I couldn't reconcile my rank. ...here I was. I was twenty, and I could sit where the governor sat. I couldn't take it...." The "Africa" he had known no longer existed for him.

Mike was a bicultural child who struggled to retain his identity. *Culture* is often considered to be an external system of customs, topography, mores, relationships, foods, celebrations, perspectives that arise out of the shared history of a people.[15] It is to be acknowledged that culture is often depicted as a "porous social reality."[16] Culture has been likened to the "humus" of a person's life.[17] Culture is seen as "the customs of particular peoples viewed as distinct self-contained wholes...."[18] The Center for Advanced Research on Language Acquisition (CARLA) has a working definition for intercultural studies: "... *culture* is defined as the shared patterns of behaviors and interactions, cognitive constructs, and affective understanding that are learned through a process of socialization. These shared patterns identify the members of a culture group while also distinguishing those of another group."[19]Culture is also an internal system that appropriates and absorbs the above. All five senses work to create this internal system which is maintained through interaction and memory.

At the time of the interview, Mike had not reached the *cultural consolidation* that is assumed in identity formation.[20] Cultural

---

[15] H. Richard Niebuhr, *Christ and Culture* (New York: Harper & Row, 1951), p.52. Culture is used by Niebuhr to refer to the secondary or artificial environment which people superimpose on the natural: language, customs, habits, social organization, ideas, etc., are involved. I am relying on this definition in addition to the interior world of the participant in culture, an interior world that is imprinted by the secondary and primary environments.

[16] Peter C. Phan, *Christianity with an Asian Face* (Maryknoll: Orbis Books, 2003), p.13: "Rather than as a sharply demarcated, self-contained, homogeneous, integrated, and integrating whole, culture today is seen as a ground of contest in relations and as a historically evolving, fragmented, inconsistent, conflicted, constructed, ever-shifting, and porous social reality."

[17] Ibid., p.18.

[18] Kathryn Tanner, *Theories of Culture: A New Agenda for Theology* (Minneapolis: Fortress Press, 1997), p.19. Tanner attributes this shift in definition to Franz Boas (1896) who introduced the German meaning of *Kultur* for the English word, *culture*. Tanner's work gives a detailed history of the meaning of "culture" into post-colonial times.

[19] Center for Advanced Research on Language (Minneapolis, MN: 2009), website.

[20] Cultural consolidation for Erikson is a "search for a new sense of continuity and sameness" with the world of skills and tools, with occupational prototypes of the day, with peers, and with the "tangible adult tasks ahead of them" (Erik Erikson,

consolidation as introduced by theorist Erik Erikson is more complex for a missionary child like Mike, a child who has been immersed in two or more cultures. For bicultural children/adolescents, the distinctness of the two or three cultures in which they have spent their adolescent formative years can result in a sense of fragmentation of their cultural identity into distinct cultural components. The cultural consolidation of which Erikson writes is much more arduous for the bicultural child. It is not impossible, it is more complicated. Cultural confusion often translated as a sense of "rootlessness" is pronounced in bicultural adolescents. Often, their cultural equilibrium is upset upon the return to the "first culture," in Mike's case, Cameroon, Africa. (See Colour Figure 1 on insert)

Cultural consolidation can be accomplished by the bicultural or tricultural adolescent or young adult. However, this process is often imbued with loss and struggle. As portraits of mature and generative bicultural adults will show, the depth of the cultural sensitivities, awareness, and intimacies far exceeds that in comparison to a person of one culture.

Margaret Mead's *Coming of Age in Samoa* was based on a study of 68 young women between ages 9 and 20.[21] In this publication of her fieldwork in Polynesia, she presented a different picture of the adolescent passage from childhood to adulthood. Mead lived in Samoa and worked through an interpreter. Her findings provoked both agreement and dissension among her colleagues. However, the most lasting legacy of this work was a clearer understanding of the impact of culture on development.

In a similar way, my life among and research of adolescents and children of missionaries away from their country of citizenship will also illustrate the impact of cultures on this passage into adulthood. I lived in Kandern, Germany, from 1976-1978, then in Basel, Switzerland, from 1978-1980, and commuted to the Black Forest Academy. In this Canadian *Internat,* I taught for four years. This "hybrid" culture has been aptly described by sociologist Ruth Hill Useem.[22] This hybrid or "third culture"

Childhood and Society (New York: W.W.Norton, 1963), p.261. In *Identity: Youth and Crisis* (New York: W.W.Norton, 1968), p.31-32, Erikson elaborated on cultural consolidation as a "newly won familiarity of the world" which prevents youth from seeing that which "might destroy this newly won familiarity of the world and expose [him] to all manner of strangeness, and above all, to the fear of death and killing.... The history of cultures, civilizations, and technologies is the history of such consolidations, while it is only in periods of marked transition that innovators appear...." (p.32) Perhaps bicultural children are these innovators!

[21] Margaret Mead, *Coming of Age in Samoa* (New York: Morrow, 1928).

[22] Ruth Hill Useem, and Richard Dixon Downie, "Third Culture Kids" in *Today's Education* (September-October 1976):103-105. See also Ruth Hill Useem, "The

[the Black Forest Academy with its dormitories] was neither German nor Canadian. I began to interview these "third culture children" [TCKs]. My methodology utilized sociological analysis, statistical analysis, historical literature, and personal narrative of 81 interviewees.[23] There were three distinct samples: 37 former inhabitants of the Basel Mission's *Kinderhaus;* 34 students and alumnae/alumni of the Black Forest Academy, a Canadian *Internat* in Kandern, Germany; a random sample of North American Protestant adult missionary children who had returned to North America. (See Colour Figure 2 on insert)

Let it be said that the bicultural child who is able to consolidate his or her cultural identity emerges as a more capable world citizen, better equipped for interpersonal and intercultural intimacy, poised for generativity, and positioned for ego integrity and leadership. It is simply a more arduous task to get there. With Eriksonian theory as a contrasting backdrop to this complexity, the narratives of bicultural children show how the circuits or "connectors" of culture impact traditional developmental theory.

American Family in India" in *The Annals of the American Academy of Political and Social Science*, Vol.368 (November 1966):132-145.

[23] In terms of methodology, this research has, heretofore, utilized sociological analysis, statistical analysis, historical literature, and personal narrative. The project has drawn primarily from eighty-one taped interviews with individuals out of three samples: thirty-seven from inhabitants of the Basel Mission's Children's Home, which closed in 1948, thirty-four students and alumnae/alumni of the Black Forest Academy, a Canadian International School in Germany, in the 1970s and 1980s; and a random sample (10) of North American Protestant overseas missionary dependents with varying ages and denominational affiliations. When this third and more current sample was augmented, *a comparative analysis* was affected between this updated and more recent group of missionary dependents and the group from the Basel Mission, a much older sampling.

The interviews were structured around fourteen questions with ample time for reflections for those being interviewed. The actual taped interviews lasted from 1.5 to 4.5 hours. The interview average was 125.7 minutes. This included the initial introduction, perusal of photos, scrapbooks, and other memorabilia.

In my dissertation, *Theological Dimensions of Maturation in a Missionary Milieu*, (Peter Lang Verlag, 1989), various hypotheses were formulated as descriptive tools. Statistical data undergirds this work. For example, Merton Strommen's Youth Research Survey, a questionnaire with 420-items and computerized results was administered to seventy-six students at the Black Forest Academy; the results were compared with 7,050 young people in a "national [USA] ecumenical sample." Using these finding and other empirical data, generally formulated problems were investigated.

It is noteworthy that traditional developmental theory is depicted in linear notions – with an upward thrust, as a ladder, a pyramid, or some structure of ascendancy. Feminists are challenging separatist linear notions of maturity and are rewriting and revisualizing development.[24] My own depiction of development has been that of a double helix, embedded in a culture(s) with interactive exchanges. In an earlier work, I illustrated physical passages for women's development in the image of the double helix.[25] In the double helix, the connectors of culture are interactive within the development of the individual. Of course, the entire developmental process is imbedded in external culture(s) as well. The internal appropriation of external stimuli and cues is represented by the "connectors" or the small bridges within the helix.

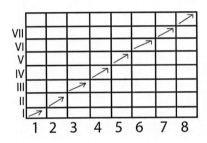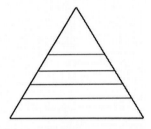

Fig. 1-1. Traditional Images of Development

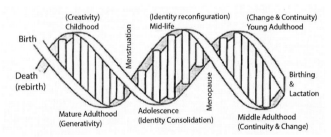

Fig. 1-2. The double helix

---

[24] *In Her Own Time: Women and Developmental Issues in Pastoral Care*, edited by Jeanne Stevenson-Moessner, (Minneapolis: Fortress Press, 2000), p.2. No one image was used in this volume, rather concentric circles (Pamela Cooper-White), tapestry (Christie Neuger), and double helix (Jeanne Stevenson-Moessner) emerge. The model was constructed to include significant physical passages for women.
[25] Ibid., p.17.

While beginning with missionary children who in their preadolescent and adolescent years were exposed to two or more cultures, this research is a study of a much larger phenomenon: the stresses, strains, and gains of bi- (or tri-) culturalism. From an anthropocentric perspective, this biculturalism has relevance for African, Hispanic, Native American, Asian American, Aboriginals, and other minorities in an Anglo culture. Building on the work of W.E.B.DuBois and his concept of "double consciousness" and Patricia Williams and her "shifting consciousness" of people of color and of women, Barbara Holmes concludes: "Despite resistance, overcoming, and the development of internal bonds of trust, and ostensible social, political, and economic advances, many African-Americans still struggle with issues of identity."[26]

The reality of the bicultural child is increasingly more obvious as children of immigrants and refugees join the voices of people of minorities who have lived "in two or more worlds." Biculturalism alters the findings within much psychological/developmental literature pertaining to childhood, adolescence, and maturity. The theory of maturation that is most closely examined in this book is that of Erik Erikson. In his psycho-social schema of maturation, the meagerness or lack of sophistication in his category of *cultural consolidation* will be highlighted. In doing so, the study of young people who are struggling to find their cultural identities in two (or more) cultures, will disclose a series of phenomena relating to home, homelessness, rootlessness, "portable roots," *cultural dissolution* [my term], and ideally – cultural resolution. The development of cultural intimacy is part of who we are. Hence, the Eriksonian stage of intimacy versus isolation is another core issue which cannot be understood without the impact of the culture(s) on intimacy.

Cultural Intimacy

Cultural intimacy is kinship to a particular form of civilization and affinity and communion through interaction with others. Religious experiences often add complexity to this process of cultural intimacy. The late David Laird Dungan, Distinguished Professor of Humanities at the University of Tennessee, Knoxville, critiqued an earlier version of my work with the following observations:

---

[26] Barbara A. Holmes, *Race and the Cosmos: An Invitation to View the World Differently* (Harrisburg: Trinity Press International, 2002), p.18. Holmes cites Du Bois, *The Souls of Black Folk* (New York: Fawcett, 1968), p.17, and Patricia Williams, "Response to Mari Matsuda: 1988 Women of Color and the Law Conference at Yale University," *Women's Rights Law Reporter* 14 (1992), p. 229.

As a missionary child myself, I have gradually learned that this religious dimension to my sense of pain and dislocation is the most important of all, both as an aspect of my religious sterility and as a path toward healing....your work will also be able to take its place beside the other studies of bi-culturalism (.... attempts at integrity or wholeness when one is irrevocably two inside). Here you will shed light on the pain and struggles of all those who have served in the military abroad and their children, Peace Corps volunteers, business families who have lived abroad, and those within the United States who move daily between one or more cultures and are part of them all.[27]

Cultural intimacy adds complexity to religious research and theological inquiry. In David Dungan's history of the Synoptic Problems, he recounted "responses to multiple, differing gospels in early Christianity" and attributed the industrious and international class at the Pontificio Instituto Biblico (part of the Universita Gregoriana) in Rome in 1976-77 as the impetus for his volume.[28] He saw how the cultural backgrounds of the students – Asian, African, Indian, European, Irish, and one American – "could predispose toward a particular hypothetical solution. I dare say this aspect of the Synoptic Problem is still unknown to me and my white, Euro-North American, male colleagues, who pay little heed to the cultural assumptions influencing their scholarly work."[29] David died in 2008. His bi-culturality prepared him to acknowledge early on in his scholarship that cultural intimacy impacts scholarly work.

The Bicultural Mind

This book offers a challenge to the traditional understanding of human development. In particular, *Portable Roots: Transplanting the Bicultural Child* underscores the contextual nature of development. The focus is on identity formation in children and adolescents who have grown up in more than one culture. Cognitive neuroscience is showing that the "bimusical

---

[27] David Laird Dungan (1936-2008), Distinguished Professor of the Humanities and Emeritus Professor of New Testament and Early Christianity, University of Tennessee, Knoxville, personal letter. David was the son of Presbyterian missionaries; he grew up in Shanghai, China, until 1940. At his sudden death in 2008, he was working on a multi media book on *Images of Jesus in Cultural Perspective*.

[28] David Laird Dungan, *A History of the Synoptic Problem: The Canon, the Text, the Composition, and the Interpretation of the Gospels* (New York: Doubleday, 1999), p.1.

[29] Ibid.

mind" reveals differences in the limbic regions of the brain and affective responses.[30] Those measuring the effects of early language learning are documenting the findings of what they term "polyglot kids." A recent study in Sweden at Lund University used brain scans to show that those learning a second language exhibited detectable growth in the hippocampus (resulting in memory and mastery of new material) and growth in three areas of the cerebral cortex (higher order reasoning).[31] The National Institutes of Health (NIH) has published studies to illustrate differences in monolingual and bilingual children, particularly in the enhanced ability of bilinguals to switch tasks more quickly.[32] As studies of the "bimusical mind" reveal more complex brain activity, as bilingualism is shown to have a wide range of cognitive advantages,[33] autobiographical ethnography is providing glimpses into the bicultural mind.[34] My work on the bicultural child discloses the more complex task of identity formation for those "intimate" from birth to late adolescence with more than one culture. One major task of "identity formation" in adolescence is that of *cultural consolidation* or a sense of "home." As my work will show, *cultural consolidation* is far more complicated for the bicultural child. My research adds the phenomenon of *cultural dissolution*, i.e., fragmentation and confusion, which precedes the stage satisfactory resolution called *cultural consolidation*. This progression of phenomena alters and amplifies traditional psycho-social developmental stages which are formed in a mono-cultural milieu.

Substantiated by my earlier empirical, quantifiable research,[35] this book contains historical narrative [thick description] or qualitative

---

[30] Wong, Patricia C.M., Chan, Alice H.D., Roy, Anil, Margulis, Elizabeth H., "The Bimusical Brain Is Not Two Monomusical Brains in One: Evidence from Musical Affective Processing," in *Journal of Cognitive Neuroscience*, 2011 Dec; vol. 23 (issue 12): 4082-93.

[31] Jeffrey Kluger. "The Power of the Bilingual Brain," in *Time,* Vol.182, No.5, 2013, p.42-47.

[32] Peggy McCardle, Ph.D., Chief of the Child Development and Behavior Branch of the NIH's Eunice Kennedy Shriver National Institute of Child Health and Human Development, spoke in a radio interview. March 8, 2012.

[33] Diaz, R. "The intellectual power of bilingualism," Q Newsletter Lab Comp Hum Cogn 1985; 7:15-22 as cited in *Journal of the American Academy of Child and Adolescent Psychiatry*, Volume 38(9), September 1999, p.1197.

[34] Manuel Pena, *Where the Ox Does Not Plow* (Albuquerque, NM: University of New Mexico Press, 2008).

[35] Jeanne Stevenson-Moessner, *Theological Dimensions in a Missionary Milieu*, op.cit.

analysis. As individuals speak about their early formative years in more than one culture, they become living human data.

A collection of essays has portrayed nomadic children as those without roots and erroneously used the image of epiphytes: "Nomadic children are like epiphytes, plants that live on moisture and nutrients in the air, blown in the wind and propped impermanently in host trees."[36] Epiphytes actually put their roots on other plants or objects as they perch there. Epiphytes can later put their roots in soil, or reverse the sequence. It is surely true that "global nomads" may not feel "rooted" in a culture, rather snatched from one place to another before roots could form. This is the life of multicultural exposures. We all have the capacity to root.

Therefore, even as I have introduced mixed images – living on a bridge, double consciousness, portable roots – I will focus on the latter. To do this, I will draw often from the discipline of botany or plant biology. I have never forgotten the pivotal interview with Edgar when he concluded: "I still have no roots." Is this even possible? Come with me now on a journey of discovery as children of two or more cultures lead us. Just as the bilingual child can switch tasks more readily than a monolingual child, just as the bimusical brain has more cognitive advantages, the bicultural child has a greater range of giftedness, resilience, and flexibility than the monocultural child. The giftedness may take various forms such as civic-mindedness, world-awareness, global sensitivities, and leadership capabilities. It is the act of transplanting from one culture to another that brings the biculturalism into stark relief. As you will see, transplanting can be a painful and risky transition. You will now hear from those of "portable roots" and see that a bicultural life is well worth living.

---

[36] *Unrooted Childhoods*, op. cit., p.1. This engaging group of narratives grew out of a Global Nomads International conference in Boston in 1994.

CHAPTER TWO

THE SOIL OF CULTURE

There was no hope ahead, so far as my eyes could see. And I was not sure whether I could enjoy the life in my own country [USA] or even adjust to it. After the years in an age-old culture [China], there were aspects of American life which seemed crude by comparison. I wondered whether I could live in so new a land, among a people so far from homogeneous. I confess to hours, even days and weeks of doubt in those first years in my own country (USA). [Pearl Buck, *For Spacious Skies*, upon her return to the USA at age 42]

Pearl Buck was born in the USA while her Presbyterian missionary parents were on furlough. She left at three months of age, not to return until she entered Randolph-Macon Woman's College (1910-1914). Pearl Buck returned to China after college and remained there until she was 42. The opening quote expresses her malaise upon transplanting to her "own country," the USA.

The Case of Edgar

The pivotal interview for my own research began with Edgar, the son of Protestant missionaries. It was Edgar who gave the image of transplanting "his roots wrapped in a burlap sack" with a little dirt brushed over the sack with each transition. Edgar grew up in a missionary culture. Edgar's father had grown up on a mission field. He followed in his parents' profession. He and his wife, both USA citizens, served in Ghana where their four children were raised. Edgar was their eldest; he was raised by two national women much of the time while his mother taught for the mission.

Edgar remembers that at five or six he was the only child his age on the mission station. By the time he was eight, he "had come to live in almost a totally book world." When he was nine years of age, he, his mother and siblings were evacuated from their home in Ghana – leaving his father behind. Edgar described this move as "disruptive" to his "world." The family was reunited in Africa when Edgar was 11 and in sixth grade. He was enrolled in a mission boarding school some distance from his parents. Every afternoon, Edgar would read and immerse himself in the delights of his book world. When he was 13 and in eighth grade, a teacher in the school was worried about his withdrawal into this "book world." The teacher communicated this concern to Edgar's parents who sent him, a year later, for testing.

Upon graduating from this mission school, Edgar won a prestigious scholarship to study at the college of his choice in the USA. He chose a small college in the southern part of the USA, near a relative. He says of his adjustment to college: "Whenever I've tried to tell my parents how terrible the *adjustment* to college was, they have just concluded that I was exaggerating." (1978 interview) In 1981, in a subsequent interview, Edgar elaborated on the adjustment:

> I went to bed at six every night. I could only tolerate being awake for 12 hours….I was psychosomatically unable to tolerate being conscious for more than twelve hours. …That was one of the worst years of adjustment to the States. I remember very little about that first year. I remember a very little bit about the classes. I remember a little bit about choir, a little bit about church, and I remember a very few things that shocked me, but I blotted out just about everything on purpose. I mean, I did not do it consciously on purpose, but I'm sure subconsciously it was quite deliberate. …You blot out certain things that are intolerable.

After college, Edgar made a "difficult" adjustment to a mainline seminary in the USA. He was able to perpetuate his secure "world of books and church" by exchanging one academic location for another. He excelled in his studies. He spent a year at a major university in Paris, an adjustment he described as "not so severe." When I first interviewed Edgar in 1978, he was in a doctoral program at a highly competitive divinity school in Boston. At the time of the first interview, Edgar had just returned from a six-week summer experience in Europe which he described as disorienting. His discomfort of moving around was noteworthy inasmuch as it contrasts with missionary dependents' desire to travel and to experience new lands and cultures.[1] In fact, research has shown the difficulty for them to settle into a career because of their aversion to a sedentary life and their wanderlust.

For Edgar, moving around only increased the sense of disorientation, of "not belonging anywhere," which he expressed in the following terms:

> I hate the fact that somehow or other, I have gotten so warped I don't fit – and will never fit – except possibly in a classroom or library. Books are the

---

[1] Jeanne Stevenson-Moessner, *Theological Dimensions of Maturation in a Missionary Milieu,* ibid.

one thing that has always been constant. ...I don't want to be an ivory tower. Part of me is afraid that might be selfish, might be escaping from the world [to which] I can't adjust. In a sense, being in a classroom is escapism.

Edgar began to feel comfortable and free to be a scholar. He was not called by God to go "traipsing across the world...."

To summarize, at a formative age, near the onset of puberty, Edgar found a certain security in a "world" buffered by books and colonnaded with church. This was his "world" on the mission field and in his mission school in Ghana as he carefully constructed it in the vulnerable years between ages eight and fourteen. Then, he lived out of this "world" and carried it around with him, locating it whenever possible in an academic setting. In the 1978 interview, when Edgar referred to this world of books and church as "living on a bridge," he was describing his inability to integrate comfortably into either culture: Ghana or the USA. (See Colour Figure 3 on insert)

In 1981, when I interviewed Edgar for the second time, he was in Europe on a scholarship to research for his dissertation. As mentioned earlier, he used the metaphor of roots packed in burlap to illustrate the *cultural dissolution* or fragmentation at that stage of his life.

Interviewer: Would you say it was a sign of an integrated personality to carry one's roots around with them?

Edgar: Yes and no. It's an integrated personality, not a socialized personality. I don't think I've ever had any identity crisis. There's no doubt in my mind who I [am], or how I was put together psychologically. ...It's always been, how do I fit who I am into the society around me, into the different societies as I encounter each one? And there I haven't done a very good job, frankly. By dint of trying to keep personality together, identity in order – that's my burlap sack, I should say – in order to keep that together, consequently, maybe almost necessarily, I could not really adjust to different societies. That would have meant untying the burlap sack and planting the roots in that society. It wouldn't have destroyed the personality, but it would have made it extremely difficult to move that personality as an integrated identity into the next society when I had to move. ...It would have been a tearing...of the character of the identity, if it had to be transplanted, if it had been properly rooted in that society....I have sacrificed integrating myself into society. I adjust. I adjust very rapidly on the surface. It's easy to brush a little dirt over the burlap sack....I carry around with me the same books, for example. I don't know how many other people have done this as consciously as I have.

Thus, in order to prevent a "tearing of the character of the identity" by integrating into society in the land of his citizenship [USA], this bicultural individual chooses to function out of a third or hybrid culture: "the world of my books and church."

Granted there are more dimensions at play in these excerpts from the interviews than the cultural dimension alone. Edgar expressed this in his own way:

> I think I would have had some of the same problems had I grown up in the States. ...I would not have had...as much sense of cultural rootlessness. I would have had some. But I don't think I would have had as much, and I wouldn't have had any sense of geographic *uprootedness*. [italics mine] Places are important to me. And there's never been any stable place....of course, if my parents had moved all over the States, I might have had some problems there, too. I can't say it is just missionary kids. I can say it seems to be more common in missionary kids.

Edgar's doctoral thesis was an extension of living in his world of books and church. He described his thesis as "close to being my family." In the 1980s, Edgar accepted a position as head librarian in a theological school; he was also asked to be an assistant professor in his theological field at this American institution, thus successfully perpetuating his "hybrid or third culture" of books and church. Edgar currently worships in an AME congregation which has primarily African-American members.

Uprootedness

In her book, *Children of the Call*, Charlene Gray describes the roots of bi-cultural children like herself as "grounded differently."[2] Born in Tanzania as the daughter of Southern Baptist missionaries, Charlene recounts the geographical and cultural shifts: "change is always looming."[3] To her, missionary children plant their roots by relationships, not location. The assimilation process works in both cultures of her life although after years in the USA, she still calls East Africa "home."

Simone Weil wrote of uprootedness in her work, *L'Enracinement* or *The Need for Roots*. Weil was born into a Jewish home, but later had a mystical experience in Assisi and became Christian. She labored for the working class of France and fought in the French Resistance. Frail all her life, she contracted tuberculosis. She spent her last days in a sanatorium in

---

[2] Charlene J. Gray, *Children of the Call: Issues Missionaries' Kids Face* (Birmingham: New Hope, 1995), p.59.
[3] Ibid.

Ashford, Kent. According to eyewitnesses, she refused to take more food than the official rations for ordinary people of France. She died in 1943 of a weakened condition leading to cardiac arrest. Before she died, she wrote about *uprootedness*.

> To be rooted is perhaps the most important and least recognized need of the human soul. It is one of the hardest to define. A human being has roots by virtue of his [her] real, active and natural participation in the life of a community which preserves in living shape certain particular treasures of the past and certain particular expectations for the future.[4]

Rootedness to her was a "vital medium."[5] Nowhere did Weil describe this more forcefully than in the image of the "soul sticking: like the skin to some burning object." She writes in the context of the fall of France to Germany in World War II. Although Weil died before *The Need for Roots* was finished or published, she left this analogy:

> Today every French [person] knows what it was he [she] missed as soon as France fell. He [she] knows it as well as he [she] knows what is missing when one is forced to go hungry. He [she] knows that one part of his [her] soul sticks so closely to France that when France is taken away it remains stuck to her, like the skin does to some burning object, and is thus pulled off. There is something, then, to which a part of every French [person's] soul sticks, and is the same for all, unique, real though impalpable, and real in the sense of something one is able to touch.[6]

How does one become rooted?

Cultural Identity

Bicultural adolescents pose questions about the balancing act of living in more than one culture. The consolidation of a cultural identity does not come easy for them. As they attempt to find their way in the disparity, hybridity, and compartmentalization of their cultures, they fall somewhere on a spectrum of cultural identity.

cultural fragmentation (dissolution) → cultural confusion → cultural consolidation

---

[4] Simone Weil, *The Need for Roots* (London: Routledge & Kegan Paul, Ltd., 1952), p. 41. Translated from *L'Enracinement,* 1949.
[5] Ibid., p.151.
[6] Ibid., p.152.

With which culture(s) do they feel most intimate? Can they move with flexibility among cultures? Are they rooted more in one particular culture? Do they feel at home in a hybrid culture? Do they feel "at home" in any one culture?

One of the most recent volumes of narratives of bicultural children contains what Gilbert Ryle introduced as *thick descriptions* or ruminations of the conquest of a problem or the acquisition of something not yet within reach.[7] It is thoughtful deliberation on "how to cross the swinging bridge." According to Ryle, thick narratives are not intended to lecture or instruct as would a teacher or to garner votes or influence as would a politician. It is to explore ground unknown to oneself. It is to grasp at mastery of something not quite within reach.[8]

One recent reflection of life by an American child raised in Korea raises the possible "fusion" of cultures[9] or of life as a cultural broker, never this culture or that. Donna Sidwell DeGracia reflects on the struggles of acculturation, periods of maladjustment, loneliness growing up between cultures, cultural separation anxiety, life in parallel cultures, life with one foot in each country. Riding in the back of a bus in the 1960s with African-Americans, she as a white girl did not know the cultural "coding" of the USA. She wonders if she is like an invisible immigrant or a virtual immigrant in her country of citizenship [USA]. This openness to reflection is what Ryle meant by "thick description." To put it another way using Donna Sidwell DeGracia's image of a traveller stuck on a "tenuous bridge," it is not an attempt to jump to one side of the bridge, rather it is a laborious balancing act to finally get "home."

In *Identity: Youth and Crisis*, Erik Erikson introduces the concept of *cultural consolidation*, defined as a "newly won familiarity of the world," with certain cultural coordinates within which individuals satisfactorily manage their lived world and are successful in daily transactions.[10] My research has shown that such a *cultural consolidation* is difficult for the bicultural (or tricultural) child, who has often been exposed to two or three cultures, unlike the children of unicultural experience, cited by Erikson. For bicultural children, who have experienced two or three cultures, I am introducing the term *cultural dissolution* which is likely to occur during

---

[7] Gilbert Ryle, "The Thinking of Thoughts: What is 'Le Penseur' Doing?" University Lectures, no.18, University of Saskatchewan, 1968. Published in *Collected Papers,* Vol. II, Hutchinson, 1971.
[8] Ibid.
[9] Sidwell DeGracia, op.cit., p.144.
[10] Erik Erikson, *Identity: Youth and Crisis* (New York: W.W. Norton & Co., 1968), p.31-32.

the adolescent stage of development. Cultural dissolution is the fragmentation of cultural identity into its distinct cultural components. The impact of various cultures on a child in his or her prepuberty, puberty, adolescent and young adult years can result in a cultural diffusion or confusion and prevent the *cultural consolidation* which is part of the ego's struggle for identity.

Erikson hypothesizes that three human processes interact to establish and maintain a person's existence as "continued in time and organized in form"[11]: the biological process, the social process, and the ego process, of which the last two concern us now.

For Erikson, the ego is an organization principle necessary for a sense of coherent personality. "What may be called the ego process is the organizational principle by which the individual maintains himself [herself] as a coherent personality with a sameness and continuity both in his [her] self-experience and in his [her] actuality for others."[12] The social process is the interpersonal interactions of the individual. "The second is the social process, by which organisms come to be organized in groups which are geographically, historically, and culturally defined."[13] This is precisely the conflict for the bicultural child, who must struggle for cultural definition with geographic repercussions. This complicates the social process, which influences the ego process. Erikson refers to the "unbroken interaction of all parts...governed by a relativity which makes each process dependent on the others. This means that any changes observed in one will cause and be influenced by changes in the others. True, each of these processes has its own warning signals: pain, anxiety, and panic. They warn of the danger of organic dysfunction, of impairment of ego mastery, and of loss of group identity; but each signal announces a threat to all."[14]

Erikson gave two examples of how cultural equilibrium had been upset, the first in victims of war [WWII], the other in victims of conquest [Sioux children]. After WWII, "identity crisis was used to describe people in rehabilitation clinics who, because of the war, had lost "a sense of sameness and historical continuity."[15] The absenteeism and emotional withdrawal of Sioux children in U.S. government schools was portrayed

---

[11] Ibid., p.73.
[12] Ibid.
[13] Ibid.
[14] Ibid.
[15] Ibid., p.17.

by Erikson as stemming from the conflict between the two worlds of the Sioux children.[16]

The cultural equilibrium is most often upset for bicultural children in their adolescent years, when they must struggle for identity with respect to their peers, who are imbedded in a particular culture. The social process is disturbed when the bicultural children find themselves unable to maintain cultural, geographic, and historical unity. The social process is interactive with the ego process. To rephrase, an inner and outer discontinuity disturb the organization of personal sameness. A sense of superiority assigned to a particular culture further jeopardizes the social identity process.

Case of Georgiana

Georgiana came to Europe from Canada at age nine and attended a small school which met in a home in Switzerland. Only other missionary children like herself were students. When her family returned to Canada, she was 15 and ready for ninth grade. Although she had made the highest marks in eighth grade, she was required to repeat eighth grade in Canada.

> Georgiana: I think the adjustments are far greater to be made going back "home" – [she asked that quotes be placed around the word "home"] – than coming to the mission field….I think it's one reason why there are so many second and third generation missionaries, because…a lot of them – it's just too difficult for them to make it back home, and they feel more comfortable in the country [in which] they have grown up…yet that's not your home either, and you really don't feel you have a home.

> When you go home, you are *totally* lost….socially and culturally, not financially….It was just such a change from a tiny, tiny private school to a huge public school, just the whole way of life, just the attitude….Plus the studies. Plus the culture shock….When you're a teenager, you already have enough. There's peer pressure, so many other pressures and struggles….

Georgiana returned for ninth, tenth, and eleventh grades at the small private mission school in Switzerland. She completed twelfth grade back in Canada. Then she attended a small Bible institute in North America, going back and forth between North America and her parents' evangelistic organization now headquartered in Germany. She fell in love with a younger student at the Bible Institute. She had prayed to marry a missionary so she could travel again. After two, almost three years of

---

[16] Erik Erikson, *Childhood and Society*, second edition, (New York: W.W.Norton & Co., 1963), p.146, 163.

marriage, she and her husband came to Germany to work in her father's organization. Later, they became independent missionaries in a parallel ministry.

Georgiana successfully returned to what has been labeled as a "third culture."[17] Sociologist Ruth Hill Useem created the term to mean "the way of life that is developed in the interstices between societies. It includes the occupational roles, languages, values, and customs that are created and shared by persons who are crossing cultural, societal or national boundary lines to relate their societies, cultures, or nations (or sections thereof) to each other."[18] In a personal letter, Ruth Hill Useem referred to the original context of the term: "The term 'third culture' was originally coined in the 1950s out of our studies of the interaction of adults from the West (mostly Americans) who had moved into India and Vietnam in the post-independence, nation-building period."[19] The term may have been coined in studies involving Vietnam and India, but the phenomenon is described in narratives from children of missionaries to other countries. Writing from her experience in Korea, Donna Sidwell DeGracia maintains that children are "more likely to absorb and internalize the culture of the host country, creating their own hybrid culture. That unique culture varied from that of their parents, the culture of the country where they grew up, and the 'home' culture to which they had to adapt as adults, making them perpetual outsiders."[20]

The term "third culture" usually designates a hybrid culture. Perhaps this is what some students experience at Miramonte Elementary School, a barrio school in south Los Angeles, where recent cases of child sexual abuse by Miramonte teachers have been reported.[21] Quoting Lisa Aronson Fontes, psychology professor at University of Massachusetts, low-income, first-generation immigrants create a particularly vulnerable situation for predators: "Families who feel disempowered in a variety of ways are going to have trouble challenging authorities like a teacher....If they're first-generation immigrants, if their English skills are limited, if they're

---

[17] Ruth Hill Useem. This concept has been augmented in the work of David C. Pollock and Ruth E. Van Reken, *Third Culture Kids: Growing Up Among Worlds*, revised edition (Boston: Nicholas Brealey, 2009).

[18] Ray Downs, "A Look at the Third Culture Child," in *Japan Christian Quarterly* Vol.42, No.2 (Spring 1976), 66.

[19] Ruth Hill Useem, personal letter to Jeanne Stevenson-Moessner, dated June 6, 1982.

[20] Donna Sidwell DeGracia, op. cit., p. 13.

[21] William Welch and Marisol Bello, "A perfect recipe for a predator" in *USA Today*, Feb.10. 2012, 1-2A.

low-income, they're going to have an even harder time challenging authority."[22]

In a way, this school which is almost 100% Latino, is a type of hybrid culture, a third culture. A majority of students come from immigrant families where English is not spoken at "home," where some parents lack legal immigrant status. Thus, the students are in a L.A. public school system which is foreign to their "home" environment, distinct from the country of origin of their parents, and isolated from diverse, mainstream American public schools in such a way that it is a barrio-school. The lack of parental involvement due to language skills, work demands, or shyness further isolates the children.[23] Thus, the children of first-generation immigrants may also experience a hybrid culture and perhaps the phenomenon of being transplanted as a bicultural child.

Case of Valerie

Valerie was born in America, but arrived in France when she was ten months of age. Although she is American, she has a French "part." She never really feels complete in either culture. There's always a part missing, she says.

As a child, Valerie was brought up speaking English at home and French in the French public schools. Her hybrid culture was that of an American Bible school environment in France. At age fourteen, she left France to attend a high school in the United States. She describes it as "not a typical American school" because of the large percentage of dependents of missionaries enrolled. Her brother was there with her the first year; that helped her orientation. She attended the highschool until she was seventeen, then returned to France. In France, she first attended an American college for two years, then the Bible school in France where her parents worked. Afterwards, she lived for a year in Switzerland where she met and dated a Frenchman. Valerie returned to the USA to finish college, in part because of the "fervent pressure" from friends and from within herself not to marry this Frenchman, who was not a Christian. Nevertheless, she did marry the Frenchman and lived with him in the USA for a while before they settled in France and owned their own business.

Valerie has been able to integrate into her second culture [France] because she was first exposed to it at an early age (10 months), because she attended French schools up to the age of fourteen, and because of her

---

[22] Ibid., p, 2A. Fontes is the author of *Child Abuse and Culture: Working with Diverse Families.*
[23] Ibid.

language facility and marriage to a Frenchman. "If I am in the United States, I have a tendency to become very French, to see and do things with a French eye. When in France, I become very American. I'm very reactionary to my environment." Being in one culture sharpens the focus of the other. "There's always a part missing."

A body of literature around the "sociology of the stranger" focuses solely on the relationship between the individual and the host community. At times, the individual is guest, sojourner, newcomer, intruder, inner enemy, marginal person.[24] The seminal work for this typology of relationships was Georg Simmel's *Soziologie*.[25] Gradations of "social distance" are given for the diverse categories and types of relationship. It is clear that "social distance" would exist in Valerie's peer groups, not only in France, but upon her return to the USA. For example, while on the mission field or in the mission school in France, she may be viewed as a "sojourner" which would be close to Simmel's concept of "stranger."[26] In her country of citizenship [USA], Valerie might be thought of as a "marginal person" or even as an "estranged native." The "marginal person" could include the position of the "homecomer."[27]

In summary, the bicultural or tricultural experience changes the child/adolescent's sociological position vis-à-vis the host community at an age when cultural identity is beginning to emerge for the child/adolescent. Bicultural mobility presents challenges not only in the way these children are perceived but in the way they perceive themselves!!

The Trembling Reed

Knit to thy heart the ties of kindred – home-
Cling to the land, the dear land of thy sires,
Grapple to that with thy whole heart and soul!
Thy power is rooted deeply and strongly here,
But in yon stranger world thou'lt stand alone,
A trembling reed beat down by every blast.[28]

---

[24] Donald Levine, "Simmel at a Distance: On the History and the Systematics of the Sociology of the Stranger," *Sociological Focus* vol.10, no.1 (January 1997), pp.15-29.

[25] Georg Simmel, *Soziologie* (Leipzig: Duncker & Humblot, 1908).

[26] Levine, op.cit., p.25.

[27] Ibid. Levine draws from the work of Alfred Schutz (1945). See also Edward A. Tiryakian (1973) and Elliott P. Skinner (1974) on "estranged native".

[28] Johann Christoph Friedrich von Schiller, *William Tell, Schauspiel* (Tuebingen: Cotta, 1804).

A sense of rootedness in the homeland, often taken for granted by those who have never experienced a loss or separation from "home," has been attested to in literature, through national celebrations, and with bursts of patriotism. The native land evokes a "personal relationship" as if it were a "living organism."[29] A homeland gives a sense of security and belonging to its citizens and in doing so, protects from isolation. "I do not wish to renounce my sense of belonging to a civic community nor the sense of security it entails, but rather, to hold these elements of life valuable, for they protect from the isolation that is so often bemoaned today and saps our best energies."[30]

It is this very sense of isolation that can create the feelings of uprootedness in bicultural children. As mentioned earlier, this is usually provoked by a return to the first culture and occurs typically in the adolescent or late adolescent stage of development in our Western cultures. The sense of cultural isolation may be accompanied by a sense of mourning for the "lost" culture in which a young person's identity was consolidating.

There are many kinds of reeds, some are cane-like perennial grasses growing 12-16 feet tall. Single reeds, double reeds, free reeds are often made into Asian musical instruments like the Chinese transverse flute. Reeds are not just willowy grasses, but are also strong bamboo stalks. What they have in common are the roots.

Uprooted bicultural children may present at times as "a trembling reed," swayed by blasts of winds of change and torrents of emotion. However, a reed is resilient and not easily broken by changes in the cultural climate. A recent compilation of reflection by bicultural authors, often called global nomads or third culture kids, echoes both the themes of rootlessness and rootedness in several cultures. There is fragility and strength in the stories. In her essay titled "Outsider," Nina Sichel states with boldness: "We are the rootless ones. Raised to believe we're of one culture, plunged into another, we sometimes wonder our whole lives long which home is truly ours. My passport identifies me as a U.S. citizen, my *cedula* [national identification card] as a resident of Venezuela. I can sing both national anthems, and feel no preference."[31] There is a nostalgia for

---

[29] Werner Schnieper, "Baslerstab Kolumne," *Baslerstab* (periodical), 31 July 1982, p.1.

[30] Ibid.

[31] Nina Sichel, "Outsider," in *Writing Out of Limbo: International Childhoods, Global Nomads and Third Culture Kids*, eds. Gene Bell-Villada and Nina Sichel with Faith Eidse and Elaine Neil Orr, (Newcastle upon Tyne: Cambridge Scholars Publishing, 2011), p.197.

home and history. Moving seven times in nine years, Nina feels like an outsider; even with a job and a boyfriend, she is isolated. In Michigan, she works with migrant farmworkers; in Miami, with Cuban refugees. Currently residing in Washington, D.C., she embraces her portable roots: "I like to be where I can find people outside the mainstream, born in one place, raised in another, not particularly interested in permanence or able to sink roots. People in transit, people who are looking for home. People like me."[32] A transplanted reed, no longer trembling.

---

[32] Ibid., p.208.

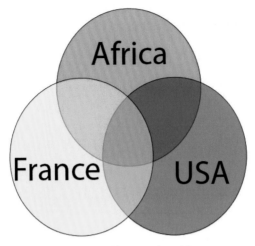

Colour Figure 1. Drawn as Mike saw his several worlds

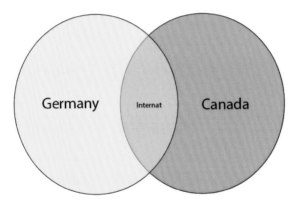

Colour Figure 2. The "hybrid" or third culture of the *Internat*

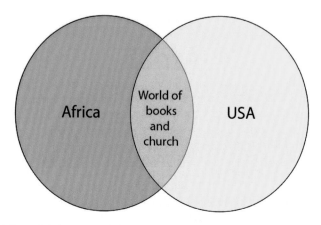

Colour Figure 3. Edgar's "world of books and church"

CHAPTER THREE

TRANSPLANTING

Grief

"Here in the Kahemba Territory of southern Democratic Republic of the Congo my missionary parents buried my umbilical cord and my heart hails home."[1] Charity Eidse Schellenberg was born in 1956 in Kahemba and was raised among the Chokwe-Lunda people. She returned to Canada for her college education, married in 1975 with the hope that she and her husband could visit Congo. Political upheaval prevented this for thirty years. In 2005, she returned for a reunion at The American School of Kinshasa (TASOK), but was grilled at the checkpoint in Kinshasa. When it was discovered that she was Chockwe, there was a warm welcome by the soldiers and guards. As her husband stated, "She was born and raised here and is returning to Congo for the first time in thirty-two years to 'nurse at her mother's breast.'"[2]

The umbilical cord of one's early formation connects that person to mother, motherland, and Mother Earth. In this honest and vulnerable account of her return to Kahemba, Charity Eidse Schellenberg, "resurrected stories from [her] youth that had atrophied below the regions of [her] consciousness."[3] This included an awareness of her romantic love for Kalema, her Chokwe boyfriend. Realizing that she was in love with two men, Charity's marriage was nearing breakdown. Upon return to Canada, Charity and her husband went through three weeks of outpatient counseling at Missionary Health Institute in Toronto. Charity was diagnosed in a regressive state stemming "from the traumatic, complete

---

[1] Charity Eidse Schellenberg, "Jubilee," in *Writing Out of Limbo: International Childhoods, Global Nomads and Third Culture Kids*, eds. Gene Bell-Villada and Nina Sichel with Faith Eidse and Elaine Neil Orr, (Newcastle upon Tyne: Cambridge Scholars Publishing, 2011), p.102.
p.102.
[2] Ibid., p.103.
[3] Ibid., p.112.

separation of [herself] from [her] formative identity."[4] She and her husband were then referred to several months of residential crisis counseling at Link Care Center in Fresno, California. In individual, group, and family therapy, she sorted through the "fragments" of her life and recovered the values on which to rebuild.[5] This is a courageous exposé of what is meant by "cultural fragmentation."

Cultural fragmentation is usually shrouded in grief. For this process of mourning, I turn to psychoanalyst Sigmund Freud. In an essay written during the destructions of World War I, Freud described a sense of grieving that invariably follows the passing of transient things. The process of mourning for familiar landscapes, the countryside, art, achievements of civilization, and other aspects of culture is, he hypothesized, the grieving of the libido over the loss of objects that were loved:

> We cannot be surprised that our libido, thus bereft of so many of its objects, has clung with all the greater intensity to what is left to us, that our love of our country, our affection for those nearest us and our pride in what is common to us have suddenly grown stronger. But have those other possessions, which we have now lost, really ceased to have any worth for us because they proved so perishable and so resistant?[6]

Freud thought not. Those who think so are simply in a "state of mourning for what is lost."[7] When the mourning runs its course, the libido is then free to replace the lost objects. "Replace" is probably not the best word to use, rather, the libido is free to reattach. For bicultural adolescents, mourning the "lost culture" can best be done with others who share the sense of loss and who can reminisce with them about the culture they loved so much. For some, delayed onset of the "mourning for the lost culture" can result in cultural confusion. For others, denial or repression of mourning can result in cultural fragmentation as we saw in Charity Eidse Schellenberg,

My questionnaires and interviews with bicultural children/adolescents showed a progression in the perception of cultural belonging – one's roots or "home." To the question, where is home, children of elementary age invariably gave a definite geographic location. But the responses of high school sophomores, juniors, and seniors (ages 15-18) tended to be less

---

[4] Ibid., p.116.
[5] Ibid.
[6] Sigmund Freud, *Character and Culture* (New York: Macmillan, 1963), p.151. Originally published as *Das Land Goethes* (Berlin, 1916).
[7] Ibid.

definite, even ambiguous: "wherever my parents are" or "both Switzerland and Nigeria" or "nowhere-everywhere" or "I don't really have a home." Cultural confusion is most fully manifest in late adolescence, with educational, vocational, and marital decisions heavily influenced by how the ambiguity is resolved. In some cases, a particular choice of partner or career itself attempts to resolve the confusion.

Identity versus identity confusion is the core task of adolescence. At least, this is the developmental stage at which the task reaches its ascendancy and urgency for a favorable resolution. The range of responses in my questionnaires and interviews fell into six categories: (1) "I am at home in both cultures." (2) "I am a torn person, my personality is being torn." (3) "I have no roots." (4) "Home is wherever I am, wherever my heart is, etc." (5) "I am at home in [name of country or place]." (6) Some combination of the preceding responses.

Responses (1) and (4) can signify a cultural adaptability that will facilitate the overarching process of identity consolidation. More often than not, such responses were given by bicultural children/adolescents who were still in the second (or third culture) and had not yet had to deal with re-entry into the passport country (first culture). Responses (2) and (3) can indicate cultural confusion, even cultural fragmentation. Inability to resolve the confusion may influence or inhibit intimacy or partnership or marriage; it also may influence career decisions. It can create a vulnerability to and debilitating sense of isolation. Response (5) was usually given by bicultural young people who had spent a preponderant amount of time in only one culture and were satisfied to remain in or return (in cases of furlough) to this culture to which they had been highly exposed. Response (6), that is, a response combining elements of the other categories, has an ambiguity of its own. Here is an example of (6) from a 21-year-old married female student:

> Home is definitely Finland. But also wherever I have to spend more than a week's time, I make my home. When I started my [degree], and my friend would ask me just to start a conversation with 'Where are you from?' – I realized I didn't know and had to answer, 'I'm from nowhere.'

To summarize, bicultural children normally go through a period of cultural rootlessness; it is often prolonged and can affect their social orientation or social location. The interplay of their field experience (in countries where their parents are stationed or serving) and their furlough time (in country of passport) only accentuates the cultural confusion. Stanley Lindquist attributes this to "the inability to put one's roots down emotionally....because of the feeling that on furlough, we will be going back, and on the field, we'll be going on furlough – not being able to identify clearly with one's own peers as children."[8]

The question of roots is a pervasive one among bicultural adolescents and adults. Only by understanding the bond to a tribe or a village or a nation can one understand its loss. Such a loss is a contributing factor to the phenomenon of cultural confusion expressed in the words: "I'm from nowhere."

White Lotus: A Longing for Home

Ruth Carson West, the adult daughter of missionaries, recommended that I read John Hersey's *White Lotus.* Ruth was born in 1922, in Hong Kong. As a child, she lived on the Cheeloo University campus in Shantung, China. John Hersey was born in June 1914 in Tientsin, China, also to missionaries. He learned to speak Chinese before English. He later became a journalist, novelist, professor; he wrote many books and won the Pulitzer Prize for *A Bell for Adano.* Ruth Carson West went to Barnard College and later completed an M.A. and a Ph.D. in special education. She returned as a missionary herself to China and the Philippines, teaching special education classes at Silliman College in the Philippines, in Malaysia, Singapore, and Bangalore, India. In reference to her work in special education, Ruth said: "You need to show a person a plausible positive way of moving from being isolated and cut off from the culture into the culture itself."

Such is the movement of Hersey's protagonist, renamed White Lotus by her Chinese owner. White Lotus, an American girl, was captured in Arizona, kidnapped along with the rest of her village, and sold by the raiders into slavery on the mainland of China. In this fiction, perhaps allegory, China won the so-called "Great War" in the time period of the 1920s. White Lotus, at only 15, was sold to various owners over a period of several years: to a middle-class mandarin, a plantation owner, a poor cotton farmer. Then she experienced freedom as a white share-cropper, to subsistence living in a silk factory in Shanghai. She summarized the initial sense of freedom in Shanghai:

> In those first days we felt free. Change is itself an illusion of freedom, but we felt more than mere escape, mere motion. Despite our having to return to the stable at evening, so to speak, we roamed at large all day, filling our

---

[8] Stanley Lindquist as quoted in Linnea Carol Larson, "A Program of Guidance in the Missionary Boarding School Based on Self-Concept System," Kansas State University thesis, 1971, p.9.

eyes, as if they were our purses, with the city's riches, and no one stopped us to identify ourselves, no one gave us patronizing looks that demanded bows or stepping aside.[9]

White Lotus tried throughout the novel to find her freedom by attaching to powerful men, also slaves like herself. She tried passive aggressiveness and became worthless to her owner; she assisted in an armed revolt; she made a run for "freedom" only to encounter impossible economic realities by first sharecropping, then by living in the big city. Although white readers like myself become aware that the African-American history in the USA is being described, John Hersey introduced this subtly as the white girl, White Lotus, was repeatedly subjugated by yellow oppressors. At the end of the novel, she was almost overpowered – until White Lotus imitated the standing posture of a sleeping bird, to shame the "yellows" into thinking she and other protesters were human. For hours, she stood on the reviewing ground in the capital of Four Rivers Province in a stand-off with His Excellency Governor K'ung. As she gave way "to a blessed sense of victory," a fear surfaced within her: what if one day "whites" are the masters, and the others are the underdogs?[10]

Why would Ruth Carson West want me to read this novel? First, the longing for home, is a central theme; in White Lotus' case, the hunger and the hankering for home [Arizona] was the foremost desire and goal in the twenty years of her life after capture. Always, she longed for home. Secondly, it is clear that only an individual with cultural dexterity could write as intimately of China as John Hersey. Ruth would recognize the "cultural intimacy" of another bicultural child, in this case, Hersey's liaison with China and the USA. Ruth mentioned to me after I had read the novel: "John Hersey came to my attention through *The New Yorker* article on Hiroshima where I had the sense of [his] intimate sharing of another culture and point of view."[11] Hersey travelled extensively in Europe and Asia and had an office in *Time's* Chongqing bureau in Southwest China (PRC). It is the pattern of a global nomad, a citizen of the world, a bicultural adult for whom *cultural consolidation* may be a lifelong journey.

---

[9] John Hersey, *White Lotus* (New York: Alfred A. Knopf, 1965), p.554.
[10] Ibid., p.683.
[11] Ruth Carson West, in a memo, May 22, 2012. Ruth is referring to John Hersey's *Hiroshima* (New York: Random House, 1946, with new edition in 1985, forty years after the explosion). The entire contents of the book appeared in *The New Yorker (*August 1946).

Ruth also saw in Hersey's work the throbbing theme of survival in an alien culture. To Ruth, that can mean "walking out of the Pyrenees in deep snow, one foot in front of the other, and with each step, expecting it to be your last. That is not hope or even a sense of a future. It is survival, and our [sophisticated] developmental tests don't even touch survival!"

Lois Dickason Young: Replanting Paradise

> I was thinking about how to describe my life…to a colleague of mine. I described it as Paradise; she said at the end: 'I don't believe you.' But it was, in many ways. I've had a lovely, lovely life. [Lois]

Sitting in Lois' living room, we enjoyed a view of her stunning garden and spring extravaganza of flowers. Like her father who had a degree in botany, Lois has a love of flora.

Like both parents, Lois has put roots down in more than one soil. Lois' interview reminded me that grief is often involved in "transplanting a life." Lois also reminded me that for the center of a plant to grow strong, it requires energy flowing from the roots to the center of the plant. A plant always needs nourishment. It can also flourish with singing and music! It needs pruning from time to time. Lois is an example of a bicultural child who has been transplanted from Burma to the USA, who has known the grief of loss, who has allowed her roots to grow offshoots, and who operates from a strong center.

Lois was born into a missionary family. Her father was an educator; her mother was an RN with a degree from Oberlin College. Lois' parents were USA citizens. They served as (American Baptist) missionaries in Burma from 1929-1966 except during their evacuation in WWII and during two years of furlough [home leave].

Asked to give a description of her life as a child of missionaries, Lois began:

> I was born in Rangoon, Burma, at home. My father taught at Judson College. My mother was a nurse. My father had many students; he taught biology, botany, zoology. He was very involved with his students and with the flora and fauna of Burma. He was always out in the hills and mountains collecting, classifying, and looking for new species; he usually had a team of students with him. He was a Scoutmaster as well. Although he taught Bible, he was not a minister. My father seemed to share his Christianity by *being*. Our house was always filled with people; they were not just Christian students, but Moslem colleagues and Buddhist friends. All types of students were welcome in our house. [My mother] worked with 'Bible women' who went with her to villages and to set up clinics in refugee

camps. Someone in the States [once remarked] that nurses on the mission field acted like doctors, and that was terrible! I answered: 'If there is no one else, what are you going to do?' [Mother] would get up in the middle of the night...for delivery of babies, lung problems, whooping cough [pertussis], and other illnesses. She taught health education classes and had glasses' clinics. She had a long-term relationship with the 'Bible Women'[12] who were her team members.

We had clinics on our back porch. Many children suffered malnutrition, and their skin would break out in sores. As part of the cure, we kids would help paint them with Gentian Violet [Methyl Violet 10B]; their skin turned temporarily purple, but the babies got better. Other babies often died at birth from malnutrition. We made coffins for these babies and lined them with my grandmother's linen napkins.

Lois witnessed loss at an early age.

Lois and her siblings were home schooled. During the war, when they were evacuated from Burma, all of the family except her father went to India. Lois was seven. Her father stayed in Burma helping to evacuate Burmese people to India. The family did not see him for about a year. Contact was occasionally made through heavily censored letters. Lois and her siblings attended boarding schools: Woodstock School in North India, then Kodaikanal School in South India. They were separated from their parents for most school years through primary and secondary grades and college.

Lois' love for Burma and for her parents was profoundly moving. She described her parents as non-judgmental and gracious. They were inclusive in their relationships and found community in the church. All four of the children have successfully found a way to transplant from the missionary home environment while honoring it. All four siblings reflect in their vocational choices the impact of a bicultural beginning. The eldest sister, six years older than Lois, became a PCUSA missionary to Ethiopia in 1953. The next sister in age entertained the idea of missions but stayed "stateside" for health reasons. She often supported international students, giving many a home away from home. The youngest sibling, a brother, is a Professor of South East Asian Studies.

Lois is third of the four siblings. She earned an RN degree at Western Reserve University, a graduate degree in special education at Columbia University, and a degree in educational administration at Bank Street College, NYC. She later began a school for dyslexic children and started a

---

[12] The Bible women were nationals who spoke the languages: for example, *karen, kachin, chin, shan.*

literacy program in prisons. She and her three siblings started the Cetana Education Foundation: Developing Human Resources through Education for Myanmar, Burma. The Foundation provides educational opportunities within the country and scholarships for Burmese students who need to study outside their country.[13] Lois is one of the founders and past President. Cetana was developed at the request of Burmese educators. This has been a meaningful way she and her siblings have connected with their parents' mission.

I asked Lois to comment on the initial adjustment from the missionary community to a wider environment. After coming to the USA for college, she didn't see her parents for four years.

> That was often painful and lonely. Twice I stole things: a pair of stockings from a girl who invited me to come home with her…once I stole $20.00 from my aunt at my grandmother's house. She knew it was me.

> Now, as an educator, I have come across examples of stealing as an expression of loss. I once knew a lonely student who stole 16 bottles of white-out. Pain and loss go together. That is what I discovered. What is isolating is when you have no one with whom to share your story. It is a solitary path when you feel lonely. The antidote, I know is to go to the garden, take a walk, or re-engage with at least one person. It is hard to do this as a younger person. It's a little different than when you are just coming out of living abroad. You don't have enough connections to know how the world works.

> When my mother died, I had a fairly severe grief response in that I was very busy, but I had this repeated dream, always that I hadn't taken care of something. The dream involved an animal that kept getting smaller and smaller. The dream was about loss. Someone said: 'You really lost your mother a long time ago when you were separated from her at an early age.'

Lois has learned in these recent years to embrace the absence of her mother in childhood. This grief as represented by the small animal in the dream was *mother loss*. I then asked where she felt "at home" in a cultural sense; she commented on the "transplanting" she experienced in returning to the USA for college.

---

[13] "Cetana ….is dedicated to helping the people of Myanmar/Burma develop future leadership by providing educational opportunities to its people without regard to religion or ethnicity, and by assisting local institutions with educational resources and professional development." From *htpp://cetana.org*.

You never do quite feel at home. You never feel fully in one place. At times, that has been more painful than others. It is very noticeable when you first come home [USA] to school. I went to the College of Wooster; my father had gone there, all my siblings attended this college, my grandmother lived there [Wooster]; we lived in Wooster during furlough years thus we did have a sense of place. This was helpful. Many of my colleagues had emotional problems, or were depressed; it was very clear that they were in a painful transition.

Transplanting roots can be a difficult task. To dig up the roots of one's identity and replant those roots in another cultural soil is an arduous undertaking. It is noteworthy that the presence of family ties in Wooster did alleviate some of the transplant shock.

Lois has managed to stay connected with her first culture, Burma. In addition to helping start the Burmese foundation (Cetana), she has made visits and taken groups to Burma.

I have taken 12 groups of people back to Burma [since 1990]. One person said: 'Well, we finally understand you.' I am generally out of sync with everybody. Not that I don't get along. I was blessed with a social personality, but I just see things differently. I used to worry about what people think. I didn't have the confidence of my convictions. I adored going back to Burma. In 1961, I took my small children, ages 2 months and two years. My parents were there, and we stayed a month. Then, we didn't go back until 1990. [weeping] You go and you just feel it's your home. When you are there awhile, you realize it was in the past, it is not the same. It is a very special connection.

Faith has also been a connection. Lois described religion as the underpinning of her life. "I see God in all people. God is more like a Friend. I happened to marry a man who was as offbeat as I am. He went to Union Seminary in NYC. He was in theatre and came from a strong Eastern family. He questioned everything....That was helpful to me in developing and stretching my faith."

I'm more inclusive and open in my faith. It is very important to me. The older I get, the more important. My sister died last August, and my husband a year ago. I miss them a lot. I was certainly upheld by my faith, by my community of faith, by individuals, and by family. I have three fabulous children and eight beautiful grandchildren who have been a huge part of my support system.

Prayer was powerful in addition to the general support. I am learning to accept the path I need to take. I think I have learned to be a better listener, than talker. At the same time, I finally found more confidence in my voice.

Lois' comfortable home was decorated with memories of her other cultures, Burma and India. She never let me forget that she had experienced transplanting. "I don't think I have ever REALLY found a home. My mother was always a doer." Lois kept active, too, until her husband suffered Parkinson's Disease and a severe stroke. Lois retired.

> I didn't stay home until I was with him. I then found staying home and being home almost seductive. I have been so active I never spent much time in the house. I wonder if it was because I never quite had a home. We lived in a number of houses as missionaries; we went to boarding school, then college. We were always moving away. Even in nursing [school] every three months, we changed our jobs. It was familiar to hear: 'Time to move.' It took me awhile to get that straightened out.

On the mission field, Lois had been taught certain cognitive coping skills. She found it hard to get in touch with her emotions upon return to the States and especially when she became a mother. Lois told the story of her daughter calling her when she [daughter] went into labor. Lois wondered why she had called her, not the doctor. Lois realized her mother was never there when she [Lois] had a baby or during many significant milestones such as plays, recitals, graduations. With her mother far away in Burma, Lois [in the USA] coped alone. "I had terrible depression after [birthing] one of my babies. I had no one to talk to about it. My husband was very busy with a production of a play, working long hours. I was loved but very alone. I didn't know other adults older than we were; others had not had my experience. I didn't know I was depressed, but I cried all the time although I had beautiful and easy children. There were times I felt alone."

A transplanted life can resemble a solitary plot of ground. Lois named it: "That piece of feeling isolated when you have nobody with whom you can share it." I often drive by Lois' house and look at the magnificence of her garden. Not all transplants would result in such fertile beds of flowers. It is an apt metaphor of the productivity, generativity, and fruitfulness of her life.

Hot House Plants

> ....he [Yuan] walked through mud and drifting rain out to the land where he had planted the foreign wheat that day. But even here there was to be no harvest, for whether the foreign wheat was not used to such long rains, or whether the black and heavy clay held the water beyond what the roots could bear, or whatever the wrong was, the foreign wheat lay rotting on the mucky earth. It had sprung up quick and tall and every seed had been alive

and swift and eager to put forth. But the earth and skies were not native to it, and it took no deep natural root, and so it lay spoiled and rotted.[14]

Before proceeding to further examples of transplanting, it is important to point out a possible difference between the bicultural experience of a dependent missionary child and that of the dependents of diplomats, military, state department personnel, or business people. The religious culture of the missionary child of theologically conservative parents, in particular, may be enclosed or sealed off from the national culture. This separation of missionary children from "contamination" by the national culture will be labeled: *cultural enclosure*. It results from a particular interpretation and application of the struggle to be "in" the world but not "of" it.[15]

An essay written by a 17-year-old student will illustrate *cultural enclosure*. After he had been caught shoplifting, this North American student was put into a conservative missionary school to separate him from his peers among the nationals. The school was also like a "hot house" for tender plants, and the school with its dormitories put him at a distance from the scene of his shoplifting. The student wrote the essay out of gratitude that he had been placed in a "stainless steel cylinder" or the conservative missionary milieu. He compared his family to a "special piece of cloth with exquisite beauty" that had been woven by God and had been stained by his acts of greed and lawlessness:

> Because my father was a missionary, we didn't have money to spare. I had now found a cheap – and for the time being – easy way of getting what I wanted. I wallowed in the filth of my sins and kept going deeper into the reeking mire….An unseen force drove me on to grab something bigger and more expensive, engraining the muddy stain deeper into God's precious cloth.

He was caught stealing radio parts. He likens this time of "being put through God's mighty washing machine." He felt that "[God] moved me to a place that could be likened to a stainless steel cylinder….."

More often than not, the North American missionary children interviewed for this research from the Black Forest Academy had been placed in this inter-mission school in order to remove them from the "secularism," "the anti-authoritarianism," the "humanistic teachings" of public school systems and the "negative influences" of their national peers. Other reasons were also given: English language education; college

---

[14] Pearl S. Buck, *A House Divided* (New York: John Day, 1935), p. 335.

[15] H. Richard Niebuhr, *Christ and Culture* (New York: Harper & Row, 1951), p.69.

preparatory work; help with the transition to their first culture [North America]. The Black Forest Academy did offer Christian instruction and perspectives, interaction with other Christians of similar age, and a "safe" environment. Unfortunately, the religious nature of the school – for some – set the school apart as a "stainless steel cylinder" in the midst of the grimy machinery of everyday living.

Needless to say, there are varying degrees of insulation. It is particularly detrimental when insulation or enclosure results from a kind of group paranoia – a fear of an impinging world of evil,[16] fear of being irresistibly drawn into this world and contaminated by it, fear of other urges felt to be uncontrollable, fear of certain quite specific elements of the world: sex, alcohol, and drugs. This can be all the more true when the staff [dorm parents, teachers], acting in *loco parentis*, assume the role of guarding the children from the external threat. Children who accept and internalize this protectionism often then feel secure in their sheltered subculture and go on to incorporate other values of their keepers. However, rebellious or irreligious students may feel cut off from collective support. "An individual feels isolated and barred from the source of collective strength when [she] (even though secretly) takes on a role considered especially evil, be it that of a drunkard or a killer, a sissy, or a sucker, or whatever colloquial designation of inferiority may be used in [her] group."[17]

Mission stations or mission boarding schools as "hot houses" are not the norm in the current climate of cultural interactivity. My examples of missionary dependents kept in isolation from the surrounding national culture or denied social interaction with nationals are from earlier decades and from conservative sending agencies. The most extreme examples I have found of keeping children away from "corrupting forces" are the following. "One person….even went so far as to imprison his children in a cage of chicken wire to keep the native [national] children from harming them from immorality."[18] Edward Danielson cites another vivid case of over-protectionism: A child's hands were regularly swabbed with alcohol to sterilize them and keep the child clean of the surrounding worldly evil.[19]

The themes of restriction and restraint appeared often enough in the literature to warrant a closer look. Restrictions took many forms: rules

---

[16] Erik Erikson, *Childhood and Society*, 2nd ed. (New York: Norton, 1963), p.36.
[17] Ibid.
[18] C. Luke Boughter, "The Family as a Missionary Unit," unpublished thesis at the Graduate School of Missions at Columbia [South Carolina], 1950, pp.61-62.
[19] Edward E. Danielson, *Missionary Kid – MK* (Pasadena, CA: Wm. Carey Library, 1984), p.24. This work was originally published in Manila, Philippines.

against dancing, the cinema, public restaurants, informal socializing with nationals, classical ballet, hand-holding, leaving the mission compound unescorted. This type of insulation can be intensified on religious/moral grounds, creating a "hot house" environment to an even greater extent for the missionary children than for the children of military, business, or diplomats. One defender of "hot house environments" argues that "we need a few more hot houses in this world, places where children won't be plagued with violence, vice and sex during those impressionable years."[20]

This is an old controversy, the theme of being in, but not of, the world. The theme has been expounded as long as "there have been sincere Christians to develop it, from as early as *The Shepherd of Hermas* and Tertullian (second century A.D.) to Leo Tolstoy and the present-day Mennonites."[21] Niebuhr further argued that a person is not only a being in culture, but a being penetrated by culture.

> If Christians do not come to Christ with the language, the thought patterns, and the moral disciplines of Judaism, they come with those of Rome; if not with those if Rome, then with those of Germany, England, Russia, America, India, or China. Hence the radical Christians are always making use of the culture, or parts of the culture, which ostensibly they reject.[22]

Some of the extreme situations presented in this last section were chosen only to illustrate that "transplanting" from a second culture or a hybrid culture will have varying degrees of difficulty depending on the child, the make-up of the child, and the milieu in which the child has been raised. Risk will always be involved, grief will be real. Many will re-root well back in the first culture [culture of citizenship/passport] as Lois did. Chapter Four will contain narratives of others who re-rooted well as bicultural children. There are many variables to this process of transplanting "portable roots." However, let us not forget that *the religious matrix* is unique to the samples of missionary dependents. Edgar, son of USA missionaries to Ghana, sums it up in this way:

> We grew up with the church as the center of our worlds…We don't belong to an irreligious world. There's nothing around us that allows us to be indifferent to religion.

---

[20] Ibid., pp.33-34.
[21] Niebuhr, op.cit.
[22] Ibid.

CHAPTER FOUR

HOLY GROUND

Theological Terrariums:
"A small, sheltered, and humble world"

Frau Roemer: I came from a small, sheltered, and humble world. And if I had stayed in it any longer, I would probably have lagged developmentally even further behind. Maybe I did get out at the right time and [that was why I] was able to make it on my own, able to make something good of my life and get my bearings again, in the world.

European missionary children in the 1930s, 1940s, who were placed in the Children's Home or *Kinderhaus* in Basel, Switzerland, were not far from their birthplaces in Germany and in Switzerland. Thirty-nine of these "adult children" of missionaries formed one of my largest samples; a significant number of these interviewees commented on a type of "enclosure" they had experienced in the Children's Home. For religious or moral reasons, the Children's Home was somewhat isolated from the mainstream culture in Basel at that time. In such a way, the Children's Home of the Basel Mission was a type of hybrid culture, neither fully Swiss nor German. The pietistic religious strain set the compound apart by a deep sense of obligation to both the mission and to the absent parents and by a myriad of expectations imposed on the missionary children.

Some of the aura of the Children's Home was skillfully captured in the book *Clouds, Wind, and Sunshine*, written by one of the interviewees.[1] This unpretentious, autobiographical work beautifully recreates the attitudes and events in the Children's Home and reveals the enthusiasm for sacrifice and separateness from worldliness.

There is no clearer example of what is meant by the term "theological terrarium" than the excerpt from a chapter titled "Much too zealous, but self-sacrificing." Pastor Arnold has just given his Sunday sermon. The example of the apostle Paul had moved the good pastor to exhortation:

---

[1] Hilde Lorch, *Wolken, Winde und Sonnenschein* (Stuttgart: Evangelische Missionsverlag, 1936). There is no English translation.

"Wait! We must change our ways. Otherwise the Lord Jesus will not have us for His service." Inspired by these words and the example of some Ephesians in Acts 19, the sisters Hanna and Elsbeth resolve to burn their "bad" books, those with the gruesome stories.

> Hanna nodded silently and Elsbeth reconstructed what was going on in Ephesus: The apostle Paul was standing in the market place. People were streaming in from the narrow alley below them. They were carrying books under their arms. A whole crowd of them. And the books contained many an evil thing. There were pictures by the Devil in them. And the people wanted to be rid of the Devil's books, because now they wanted to belong to the Lord Jesus. So they built a great bonfire and threw the books in and burned them.[2]

From their book of fairy tales had come such "wicked" stories as "The Witches' Ride to the North Pole" and "The Devil on Cuckoo Mountain." These stories and others were sacrificed as a burnt offering. "[Not even] the smallest picture would make them think of the Evil One any longer, because they would now belong in Christ Jesus' service."[3]

The pious, protected world of the Children's Home is seen positively in *Clouds, Wind, and Sunshine.* Most of those interviewed, however, regretted that the atmosphere of the Home prevented them from making the easy transition they would have liked into peer groups outside the mission compound. Transplanting was not easy.

The title of this book is *Portable Roots,* and the research draws insights from the field of botany. It is helpful to note that some plants are transplanted with little success. A transplant is a lifting of the plant from its familiar ground; the root structure is usually broken. Of course, this transplanting can result in a better fibrous root system and a stronger plant. However, any serious gardener will alert you to variable weather conditions, different soil conditions, the threat of late frost, and the matter of timing. It is best to transplant seedlings from the green house to a garden when they are in a period of dormancy. Many gardeners gradually transition their young plants or seedlings in gradations, carefully placing these young plants in small containers or planters and setting them – with increased exposure – to sun and the new climate. These young transplants can experience leaf burn, frost, and humidity shock! In a similar fashion, children who have grown up in a greenhouse or terrarium can also suffer destructive effects of a shift in the cultural soil of their young lives.

---

[2] Ibid., p.106.
[3] Ibid., p.110.

The theology of a community can create a partly or entirely closed system. That is why the metaphor of "theological terrarium" as a miniature and contained landscape is an apt one for such a milieu as the Basel Children's Home. This metaphor is not meant as a phrase of judgment, rather it is a descriptive metaphor to underscore the complexity and risk in transplanting young lives outside the closed system.

35 of my 39 interviewees reported common effects of this "theological terrarium." This response amounted to a general finding. First, many inhabitants felt themselves somehow stamped or marked as different from their peers outside the Children's Home. Sometimes this was seen as a desirable occurrence, as for example, in the book *Clouds, Wind, and Sunshine*: "Missionary folk must be brave." Most of those interviewed reported that labels such as "those poor missionary kids" had prevented them from relating or transplanting easily to peer groups outside the mission compound. Secondly, there was a strong, common bonding among the missionary children themselves, as witnessed even today in the continuing contacts and reunions of former Children's Home inhabitants. This bonding also included siblings who lived together in the Children's Home. Third, a catalyst of some kind was often used to ease the transition from the "small, sheltered world" of the Children's Home to the great world outside. The following life history will illustrate these three themes before they are dealt with separately.

Doris: "We were somehow stamped"

Doris was seven years old when she was placed in the Basel Mission's Children's Home. She had lived with her parents for four years in China, then three years in Germany with them while they were on furlough. She had difficulty in making the adjustment from the freedom she had enjoyed in China and in Germany to what she described as the confined or "hemmed in" and unnatural life of the Basel Children's Home. She recounted how the mission children were unable to socialize or play with those outside of the mission. Doris felt she bore the stamp of being a poor missionary child: "That feeling I always have. We are poor!" She remembered that due to their limited finances, the missionary children did not attend cultural activities with the exception of the patriotic drama *William Tell*. Doris described the labeling or stigmatization process as "being stamped." "Yes, we were somehow stamped. And I really believe that if a person was already inclined to feel inferior, they got a bad inferiority complex. And if a person didn't already have one, then they got one anyway."

Doris married at age 34 and in the early part of her marriage, it was difficult for her to go out to restaurants with her husband's associates and their wives. The dancing and the socializing made her uncomfortable:

> I thought that when people looked at me, they saw me as just a poor missionary child, and it made me feel so awkward. I couldn't talk with them. On the other hand, I saw they were not bad people. I really had problems.

In working through her problems, Doris utilized the reunions of the Children's Home inhabitants. The reunions were therapeutic. "You were not all alone, with all the misgivings you had. You had thought, 'the others at the reunion won't say anything' or 'they don't think like me.'" However, the theme of community bonding was recurrent in Doris' interview. She knows that if she needed help, she could knock on the door of any one of the former inhabitants of the Children's Home and receive help. The inhabitants were all like children "who have parents and yet don't have parents." Because of this parental absence, they are "like brothers and sisters who grow up alone together."

Doris is particularly close to her biological brother who also lived in the Children's Home. In her adult life, this brother settled Doris and her family near him and gave her an apartment as a gift. He said it was in honor of their parents. "It goes without saying that this feeling of being responsible for others – especially the brothers and sisters who were together in the Children's Home – is somehow unique." In contrast, Doris does not feel close to her sister who did not live in the Children's Home.

Doris' husband served as a catalyst for her transition to a freer world than her constricted life as a missionary daughter. She felt "freed" by her husband's influence. "When I got to know my husband, I first got to know what freedom there really is in the Christian faith."

In summary, Doris had mixed feelings about the overall effects on her development due to the many years she spent in the Children's Home. On the one hand, she acquired an ability to adapt to physical circumstances and the agility to enter into a Christian "community" quite easily. On the other hand, due to the simple life and the pious nature of the Children's Home "community," she felt she belonged to a different, second-class group, unlike her public school classmates who were daughters of prominent Basel families:

> I can adjust to every situation. I can live without comforts and luxuries. Somebody like me gets to feel at home in a Christian community, having come from a community the way I did. When you've once lived in a community out of necessity, it's easier to be part of a 'community' again,

easier than if you had always been protected and secure as in a nuclear family.

Doris saw the advantages to being in this "community" with its blessings of comfort and understanding given by other children whose parents were also far away at a letter's end, who also cried in bed at night thinking of Mommy and Daddy, and who instinctively formed a support group. These advantages counterbalanced the feelings of being "set apart," differentiated from contemporaries in public school, distinguished by the outward manifestations of their missionary upbringing and by their inner world. Doris articulated all three themes of moving from a terrarium or enclosed world to a larger one: labeling, bonding, and a transitional catalyst.

Greenhouses

When I speak of my research that involved former inhabitants of the Basel Mission's Children's Home, I often get the response: "That was a different time." It is true that my interviewees lived in this compound in the 1930s and 1940s. Because of World War II, the Children's Home was closed in 1948 as most missionaries came home to Europe. My sample of children of American missionaries is a more recent sample, dating from the 1980s to the present. However, there are four common themes which emerge despite the variance in time: labeling by outside peers and possible stigmatization, bonding with inside peers, transition with difficulty to a wider world, and help from a catalyst in this complicated transition. These themes also emerge today when children move from one culture to another. It can happen to children of refugees, immigrants, expatriates.

In some ways, my samples will bring these four themes into sharper focus because they present the themes in a full-blown way. The religious landscape of the missionary compounds was predominantly conservative, pietistic, and evangelical terrain. Care was taken to develop extremely rich and deep religious root systems. However, the "greenhouse" effect of the subcultural enclosure, I believe, made the transition to the world outside the enclosure more dramatic and risky. There was little cultural cross-pollination. To be labeled as "other" is as detrimental as a late frost on a transplanted seedling. To be called "a moron" is worse than humidity shock on a young sapling. Here are the stories: they reveal older time periods, but current themes.

Stories from the Children's Home

The children from the Basel Children's Home felt they had stood out
socially by virtue of their upbringing in pietistic surroundings. This was
felt most keenly in the way they dressed, by their lack of spending money,
by their minimal participation in extracurricular activities at school, by the
food they took on school outings. A number of the interviewees included
elaborate descriptions of the clothes they were given to wear. The detail of
shoes, stockings, and other apparel is not so important as the impact of this
outdated clothing at a developmental time when being like peers is
significant.

One interviewee described her embarrassment and shame. Frau
Weber's parents had outfitted her with new clothes before she entered the
Children's Home. When these clothes were outgrown, she was given
"hand-me-downs" that often really did not fit. The mission personnel told
her that looking attractive was not important. When she boldly mentioned
that a dress was too large and needed a belt, she was told she had no need
to "look slim." Frau Weber asserted: "You know, that's hard for a young
girl of 14 or 15." She attended a high school (*eine Toechterschule)* which
enrolled girls from all social circles, including the "best" or well-to-do
families in Basel. Frau Weber was so embarrassed about her clothes that
she would hide in the bathroom over recess.

The story was representative of many others. Sometimes it was shoes
that were too big or stockings that were baggy. Sometimes it was the
simple lunch they took on school outings compared to the picnic baskets
with chicken that other schoolmates had. The children from the Home
always knew they were different. They did not fit in or could not blend in
with other groups of school children.

One former inhabitant of the Children's Home painfully recalled the
social distinctions he felt, especially as reflected negatively on his parents.
He lived in the Home from age eight to twelve.

It was never made explicit, but people could tell we were missionary
children by our clothes, our pants, our shoes. This made it appear to
everybody as if we weren't cared for by our parents. As children, this
weighed on us. Comparisons were made all through school. Later, when
my parents did return from the mission field, we children were marked by
having to depend on outside assistance. These are not the easiest years to
recall, when a child is sensitive and notices how others are looking at him.
Yet if I have given the impression that these circumstances were a
disadvantage, I'd like to correct that. In later years we [children] found that
these experiences made us better able to understand people in similar
situations....We could be more attentive and serious with them. In that

way, those childhood years were an advantage. However, I have preferred not to tell my own children about them.

Although he was not a child of the Basel Mission's Children's Home, Carl Gustav Jung was the son of a pastor in Basel. This theme of "being labeled" is also mentioned by C. J. Jung in his autobiography.[4] When Jung was eleven years old (1886), he was sent to the Basel secondary school or *Gymnasium*. It is interesting to compare his experience of being different to that of the inhabitants of the Home. He described the stigma of "being poor."

> I was taken away from my rustic playmates and truly entered the "great world," where powerful personages, far more powerful than my father, lived in big, splendid houses, drove about in expensive carriages drawn by magnificent horses, and talked a refined German and French. Their sons, well dressed, equipped with fine manners and plenty of pocket money, were now my classmates. With great astonishment and a horrible secret envy, I heard them tell about their vacations in the Alps.

Jung was "flabbergasted" that his classmates had also been to the seashore! Then he became aware for the first time how poor he and his family were. "….my father was a poor country parson, and that I was a still poorer parson's son who had holes in his shoes and who had to sit in school for six hours with wet socks."[5]

Jung wrote of the feeling he had in Basel of "being classified" as belonging to a particular group. Using the same words as Doris, he wrote that he felt "stamped" because of who his father and grandfather were. He was glad to get away from Basel and assume a position as assistant at the Burghoelzli Mental Hospital in Zurich in 1990. His friends could not understand why he would leave Basel, and they predicted Jung would be back. That was out of the question, he said, "for in Basel I was stamped for all time as the son of the Reverend Paul Jung and the grandson of Professor Carl Gustav Jung."[6] He resisted returning because he refused to be "classified," and the pressure of family tradition was too great.

Hermann Hesse, a well-known inhabitant of the Basel Mission Children's Home, expressed similar sentiments. Hesse's pietistic father and grandfather were both missionaries. His father, Johannes Hesse, trained at the Basel Mission and later served in India. After Johannes

---

[4] Carl Gustav Jung, *Erinnerungen, Traume, Gedanken* (Zurich: Rascher, 1963), p.40.
[5] Ibid., p.40.
[6] Ibid., p.133.

returned to Switzerland for reasons of climate, he married, had children, and moved to Basel. Hermann Hesse was four years old at the time of the move. At age seven Hermann Hesse was placed into the Boys' House of the Basel Mission. He only lasted six months as a boarder. He was asked to leave because of his incalcitrant spirit. That was why his parents put him there in the first place.

The character Peter Camenzind in Hesse's novel of the same name, also spends a long period of time in Basel.[7] Hesse wrote the book in 1904, when he was 27, and it is assumed to contain autobiographical elements. As a young boy, the character Peter has difficulty in relating to people. As a student in Zuerich, he feels inferior. He is awkward in his relations with the female sex. Peter speaks with awe about a student, Richard, a student acquaintance in Zuerich: "I was fascinated [by Richard] but I kept my distance. I was afraid of making the acquaintance of someone so easygoing, free, and well-to-do, fearing it would only humiliate me and underscore my poverty and rough manners."[8]

Later, in Basel, Peter is advised by a physician to seek out company lest he become unbalanced. Peter enters academic circles and is invited into a professor's home. Peter prefers the company of a poor carpenter and a misshapen dwarf: "[They] sense soon enough that I was a gentleman in appearance only and basically a farmer's son and the child of ordinary people, and so that first evening we were already on good terms. For just as they recognized in me their equal, I recognized my native atmosphere in this poor household."[9]

Hermann Hesse's position in relation to society has been described as that of an "outsider."[10] He has been further described as a "romantic outsider," one who dreams of other worlds of which he is not a part.[11] Hesse later portrayed his character Steppenwolf as his most striking outsider.[12] In a letter dated February 27, 1956, Hesse wrote to Hans Mosser: "I love outsiders and am one myself."[13]

---

[7] Hermann Hesse, *Peter Camenzind*, tr. Michael Roloff (New York: Farrar, Straus and Giroux, 1969).

[8] Ibid., p.50.

[9] Ibid., p.152.

[10] Carlee Marrer-Tising, *The Reception of Hermann Hesse by the Youth in the U.S.: A Thematic Analysis,* (Bern: Peter Lang Verlag, 1982).

[11] Colin Wilson, *The Outsider* (London: V. Gollanz, 1956).

[12] Op.cit., p.192).

[13] Hermann Hesse, *Briefe-Erweiterte Ausgabe* (Frankfurt am Main: Suhrkamp Verlag, 1964), p.463.

North American Sampling:
"Certain people thought we were morons"

The North American sample encountered "labeling" and/or stigmatization most acutely when they returned to their first culture, North America. Their North American peers let them know they were "funny" or "different." Some interviewees resented the fact that their home churches presented and idealized them as "a model child," "as a fine young man/women," a member of "a sweet family," the daughter of a [well-known evangelist], as "the missionary child who can speak German" [or any other language], and so on. Such idealization and labeling created an immediate social gap for many returning adolescents, a gap that hindered them from adapting readily to their home culture.

One missionary son, now in his twenties and married, described how he experienced this social gap when he and his sister returned with the family on furlough:

> We – my sister and I – had it much harder. We suffered more at the hands of Christians, in terms of cultural rejection, mocking, things like that. Perhaps the only pointer I would give my parents now is that they should have told us more about baseball, for example. I used to get trapped into saying dirty words, and I didn't know what I was saying. I know certain people thought we were morons, because there were certain things we just didn't know, things that any American kid would know.

Thus, at a stage of development when it is important to be labeled as "insiders," many in the sampling of missionary dependents who returned to their first culture were categorized as "outsiders." This came at a time in their development when solidarity with peers is crucial to self-image. The phenomenon of labeling others is a psychological tactic by the "insiders" to strengthen their group's identity and cohesiveness by rejecting others who are "different," hence "outsiders." Labeling can also be a technique of harassment and bullying.

One missionary son whose parents served in Indonesia, described his social relocation to Canada, the country where his mother was a citizen. At the time of the interview, he was 29 years of age. He recalled the painful re-entry to Canada. He and his siblings dressed differently, having lived in Indonesia. Some students at his large Canadian public high school of 4,000 students decided to raid his locker and throw all his clothes out on the floor. He began to develop a persistent sense of inferiority. His older sister, also ridiculed for being so "different," spent half of that school year in bed, incapacitated by headaches.

Negative branding is a means a group can use to maintain internal cohesiveness and stasis. It can also produce solidarity among the outsiders. Unfortunately, religious institutions can be guilty of labeling and stigmatizing. One female inhabitant of the Basel Children's Home recalls being treated by the staff as "the scapegoat" (*der Suendenbock*). Other interviewees spontaneously confirmed this designation: "When anything at all was amiss, they would say [name of female] was involved." One result was the formation of a tightly supportive community among the young female and her four siblings.

In summary, finding oneself labeled and "branded" can provoke a variety of reactions. At the psycho-social stage of development for which belonging to a peer group is vital, it is easy to understand why bicultural young people would seek out and come together with others "like us." This brings us to the reaction of bonding.

Bonding

Understandably, bicultural children and adolescents tend to bond together when they find themselves as "outsiders" or in a new culture. They are drawn together to share the "world(s)" they have experienced. They gravitate towards one another because they have experienced more than one culture. In both my European sample [Basel Mission's Children's Home or *Kinderhaus*] and the North American sample as well as a miscellaneous sample, the theme of bonding with those who shared their "world" was dominant. This bonding was most acutely felt by those leaving a familiar culture for another.

The Case of Pia

Pia spent the first three years of her life in a jungle in Indonesia. With the exception of two furloughs, she lived all her childhood and part of her adolescence in various parts of Indonesia. Her mother home-schooled her through correspondence courses. Her parents insisted that she and her four brothers keep a certain social distance from the nationals. A tutor came to the mission field and helped with her eighth-grade course work. After her father experienced an emotional breakdown, the family returned to his homeland in Europe.

For two years, Pia attended a private Canadian school for children of missionaries. It began as a small school in a private home and later expanded to become the Black Forest Academy in Kandern, Germany. Even in this private school, Pia was conscious of having to make transitions. At 13 and 14 years of age, she was quite self-conscious of the conservative, grey clothes her mother and aunt had her wear.

When her father recuperated, the family moved to Canada, her mother's homeland. There Pia enrolled in a large public high school of 4,000 students who would laugh at her because she was so different: different in her dress, her faith, and her behavior. She found it difficult to be in a classroom with others, and even today, has a hard time "getting into a discussion or conversation with others." Pia remarked: "It's always been threatening to me. I could never ask questions in class." More than her siblings, Pia suffered academically. The high school principal assured her she would never graduate from college. She did not test well on standardized tests. For her senior year of high school, she went to a small Christian school of 300 students; people were kind to her there. With the help of her guidance counselor, she was accepted by a small Christian college. Contrary to the predictions of the standardized tests and her former principal, she made it through four years of college. Pia attributes her success in part to the other children of missionaries on campus. They "stuck together." They did not want to forget their past, rather embrace it. The students formed a club and met monthly. They shared meals together and cooked international dinners representing the countries in which they had lived. They gave a chapel service and invited missionaries to address the whole student body. The bonding of these bicultural children formed a secure support system for Pia.

In addition to these peers, Pia stayed "very close" to her family. Helped by her brothers, Pia manages an extension of her father's ministry in Europe, an ecumenical center that receives individuals and welcomes Christian conferences. At the time of the interview, Pia felt bonded to her parents, her siblings, and to other bicultural children like herself.

The Case of Karen and Robert

Karen and Robert were two "rebellious" missionary children caught up in a web of ambivalent dynamics with both their families. Karen and Robert were both extremely close to their siblings, with one exception. Karen had lived with Robert's brother for a while before she married Robert. Karen had known both Robert and his brother when they were all together in a school for children of missionaries.

Robert's sister, to whom he had been unusually close, died of a preventable disease when the religious group to which she belonged failed to take certain medical precautions before travelling to underdeveloped nations. Robert became scarred by what he considered his sister's "unnecessary death" and came to feel quite bitter about Christianity in general.

Robert is working for a firm that specializes in stained-glass windows for churches. In this way, he is able to concern himself with making church exteriors more beautiful while detaching himself from the "ugliness" of institutional Christianity. Robert recalled a rebellious episode when he was 16 and ran away from home. "My parents kept threatening to put me in a psychiatric facility. So one day I just put out my thumb and was gone for a month – to Toledo, to Ohio, to Atlanta. I slept out on the streets and in abandoned apartment buildings. I went down to Florida. I travelled around a lot. Then, I went back home after that. And they greeted me. I sat down at the table and finished dinner with them."

Karen added: "As if he had never been gone." And Robert echoed that astounding fact: "As if I had never been gone." The pain and anger that he demonstrated was never acknowledged.

Karen and Robert have settled into what used to be his grandparents' house. It is owned by his parents who live three miles away. Karen and Robert are trying to make a place for themselves in a town that has not, so far, quite managed to accept them. Karen feels judged by both the local pastor and his wife who are friends of her in-laws. Karen is uncomfortable with her in-laws: "I wonder if they see me as something I shouldn't be."

In summary, Karen and Robert are two "rebellious" bicultural young people, clinging to each other and their shared experiences, living conveniently albeit uneasily near Robert's parents who own their house. They continue trying to establish who they are vis-à-vis their families and their community.

Patterns of bonding within families (parents, siblings, in-laws) as well as with other biculturals were repeatedly recurrent in interviews. The bonding of biculturals in boarding schools and on the mission field was most acute upon their return to the first culture. This phenomenon was researched and documented by Richard Downie.[14]

Regarding bonding, there was one striking difference between the former inhabitants of the Basel Mission's Children's Home and the North American sample. The Children's Home sample also showed a high degree of bonding with peers and were able to preserve dimensions of that bonding through reunions. In comparing the two samples, however, missionary dependents who lost or left a second or hybrid culture clung more closely to other missionary dependents upon their return to the first

---

[14] Richard Downie, "Re-entry Experience and Identity Formation of Third Culture Experienced Dependent American Youth: An Exploratory Study," Michigan State University dissertation, 1976.

or home culture whereas the Children's Home inhabitants generally clung closer in adult years to their own siblings. During the absence of their parents from three to eight years (ten years when war prevented their return), the siblings became the family unit. In this reconfiguration, the parents were idealized as the separated children gazed upon their portraits, read their letters, and tried to remember them. This absence made furloughs often difficult, for the parents were not the ideal people "remembered" by the children. When the parents finally returned to Europe and tried to reassemble the family unit, readjustment was not so easy. Some former missionary children, now adults, gave evidence of a search for the reconstructed family, sometimes with their own sons and daughters, sometimes by seeing to it that their parents are now part of their adult lives. This tendency was most pronounced in former Children's Home inhabitants when the separations from parents had been particularly severe.

The Case of Simeon

Simeon, the second of three children, was born in Borneo. He lived there until he was seven, at which time he was put in the *Children's Home*. He stayed there for five years until he turned twelve. Simeon was with his elder brother.

When Simeon was twelve, his parents returned on a furlough. Simeon remembers this as a difficult time not only because of the years of separation, but because he was in puberty. Puberty was a natural, developmental time in which "you set yourself against your parents." Simeon conceded the fact that none of them knew each other very well after five years apart; this may have added to the difficulty of adjusting to life together again.

> Above all, the five-year separation from our parents meant we now had to work out a personal relationship with our parents and that they had to develop a new relationship with us....when our parents were greeted at the Basel train station upon their return in 1937, we, the children, were made the center of attention. And we immediately disappointed our parents deeply by calling them "Uncle" and "Aunt," the way we had learned to address adults in the mission compound during the five years we were separated.

When the year's furlough ended, Simeon and his brother were put in the care of foster parents. This home did not turn out to be what the parents had expected. Simeon was later sent to live with his grandparents where he took an apprenticeship. He was drafted into the military during World War II and then became a prisoner-of-war for two years.

This period in captivity and the later reunion with his parents after the war had a profound effect on Simeon's religious beliefs. He was 22 at the time. He felt that both he and his parents had been protected by grace. In a world restored to order, his religious orientation *revived*.

Fig. 4-1. Basel Mission Children's Home: A brother comforting his sister after parents' departure

Fig. 4-2. Basel Mission Children's Home: A close friendship between two girls

Simeon's parents now wanted him to become a missionary. He resisted the suggestion because he did not want to re-experience the loneliness again of being separated from his parents, or from his future children. When I asked him where his roots were, Simeon replied without hesitation: "There's no doubt about it, right here in my family." The close atmosphere was indeed evident. Simeon is extremely close to his own five children (all adolescents or young adults at the time of the interview) as he was to his parents while they were still alive. The year after Simeon married, he invited his parents to move into his house. They lived there until they *die*d – 15 and 21 years later. Simeon recalled these years as a pleasant time of "life together." Simeon had one or both parents under his roof from the time he was 29 until he was 56. He was able to create "a life together" that would not recapitulate the early years of separation from his parents, but would create a bonding with them that he so deeply needed.

In the years of conducting this research I was spontaneously handed two photographs of children from the Children's Home. They speak eloquently and pictorially of the bonding among Children's Home siblings, particularly the photo of the brother comforting his sister under an umbrella after their parents' departure. The second photo is no less expressive of the special bonding (*die Kameradschaft*) that developed among the Children's Home peers. Noticeably absent in both pictures are the parents!

The Case of Frau Mueller

Of all the interviewees, the following undoubtedly required the most courage to tell her story. At the time I met her, she was in middle age and a patient in a psychiatric clinic. She told me her life history with frankness and retrospective insight, gained from therapy. The striking theme was that of companionship (*die Kameradschaft*): in kindergarten, in Holland, in the Children's Home, as an *au pair*,[15] in a home economics course, in the psychiatric hospital. The interviewee lived without her parents in the Children's Home from age six to fifteen; her sister was seven, her brother was four when they were left alone there. The interviewee revealed the inability of her ego to develop a needed independence (*die Selbstaendigkeit*). The peer-sibling bonding was so intense in her life from age 6 through 15, that she illustrates the ego's dependency on peer bonding for ego identification. She felt she had not developed individual ego-strength. Here is her story.

Frau Mueller was born in Borneo where she lived until three and a half years of age. She and her family then moved to Holland for half a year so that their missionary father could learn Dutch. She had close friends in

---

[15] *Au pair* is a widely used French term for a foreign girl who shares in the household chores of the home into which she is invited, in return for her room and board and, hopefully, a chance to learn the local language.

Kindergarten and enjoyed it. After this short stay in Holland, the family moved to Switzerland and eventually lived in the bookshop of the Basel Mission for a year.

> And then my parents went abroad again. We were inconsolable our first day alone in the Children's Home. It was so terrible for us. We were so homesick for our parents. People tried to comfort us, with cookies and conversation. By evening, we had already settled in a bit. For the next four years, approximately, we were in contact with our parents. Then the war between the Japanese and the Dutch broke out, and our parents were imprisoned by the Japanese. We didn't know that. We just heard absolutely nothing more from our parents. But we had really gotten used to the Children's Home, and we were happy there. People really looked after us and were good to us.

Frau Mueller was nine at the time she stopped hearing from her parents. She was fourteen when they were released and came back to Switzerland. "At first, we two sisters kept praying that our parents could come back soon so that we could all be together again. But, then, as the war went on, things were different. And later we aren't [sic] homesick any more." Frau Mueller occasionally switched from the past verb tense to the present verb tense, still referring to the past. Other interviewees used terminology of the past such as the names of places; an example is the "Gold Coast" of Africa which is an outdated nomenclature.

I asked Frau Mueller more about the lack of homesickness. She reconfirmed that after several years she didn't miss her parents any more. "We felt very safe and then, too, we received lots of love from our house parents and governesses. We had good companionship. We had good friends. Oh, we had some bad governesses, once or twice, who smoked or things like that. [Smoking] wasn't yet acceptable. But most of the time we have [sic] good governesses."

After the parents were released from captivity, they returned to Basel and attempted family life together. Frau Mueller admitted that attempt did not turn out very well. Frau Mueller: "A lot of children don't get along with their parents, or the parents with their children. We'd grown too different. We'd drifted away from each other. You know, it was really not very pleasant with our parents. I would gladly have stayed on in the Children's Home."

Frau Mueller attended a public school for girls (*eine Maedchenrealschule*). Then she found a good position outside Switzerland as an *au pair*. After this positive experience, she returned to Switzerland to take the qualifying examination for certification as a kindergarten teacher. She failed the exam and was advised to enter a home economics course.

She completed the home economics program and made some nice friends. She was active in her profession for ten years.

> During those ten years, I helped raise groups of children in a number of different children's homes and in a few private families with four or more children. I like that best – the private families – because you had a mother there who could have the last word when it was needed. In the children's homes, I always felt a little bewildered. I guess I really did a few stupid things with the children when I found they were being raised too strictly. We'd had such a nice close atmosphere in our Children's Home [in Basel], so I really couldn't understand why the children should be brought up so strictly in other children's homes.

There were two such homes where she felt the severity. She began to have problems with her nerves. She described herself as "mentally ill" and speculated on the contributors to the illness: parental separation, life with her parents after their return, the lack of close friends after she left the Children's Home. "It was simply too much to go from our large band of friends in the Basel Mission Children's Home back into our small little family. We didn't get along well – my parents with us children – or we children with each other."

Frau Mueller had been told that it would be so wonderful when the parents returned. This was not the case. Frau Mueller found that she could not carry on in her profession. "It took too much out of me, what with my nerves." She worked in a small manufacturing plant for a year for a change of place. This was still too much stress for her. Looking back, she recalled the time as *au pair* as her happiest position.

At age 29, Frau Mueller entered a psychiatric facility, unable to function on her own. She described herself as depressed and disoriented, unable to make sense of the world any more. The relationship with her parents had deteriorated. She was hospitalized for a year. In the facility, she was eventually able to find not only a supportive peer group but an understanding authority structure. At the time of the interview, Frau Mueller was an outpatient, yet still referred to the facility as "here." Frau Mueller has been readmitted to the hospital at regular intervals. At first she did not like the hospital, because she felt it was too strict and confining. Eventually, she became happy in the hospital and found people very good to her. She described it as a "holiday" where she could relax. As an outpatient now, whenever she has a severe depression, she goes back right away of her own accord to the hospital. "People have such a good cheerful spirit here. Now I really only function here. What will come later, I don't know."

She mentioned that her mother had been ill with depression when she returned from Borneo. "....my mother was sad a lot of the time when she got back from the tropics, and I sort of felt influenced. It got on my nerves. I was with my sick mother from when I was 20 until I was 30. That's what made me ill. And my brother and sister and I didn't understand each other. I understood my little brother the best. He was born in Borneo, too."

I inquired if she had experienced depression in the Children's Home. She said she had not experienced depression there; the illness surfaced when she about 29. It progressed until she was hospitalized. She feels safe in the hospital. "It's better for us here when we're not so well. We don't fit in with what you'd call 'normal people' any more. They expect too much....and they don't really pay us any attention."

In closing, Frau Mueller reconfirmed her close ties with the former inhabitants of the Children's Home. "Yes, there is a strong bond there of companionship. I felt so sad when I had to be alone with just my brother and sister. In the Children's Home, I was always with four other girls the same age as I was. I never had the feeling I was alone then. We were together. We played a lot. It was fun for us at the Children's Home."

Transition and the Catalyst

The bonding which occurs among children in a home like the Basel Children's Home and among bicultural children/adolescents in other enclosed environments makes it hard for them to transition outside the familiar. Often this period of transition was described as a painful one. Three questions on the questionnaire used in this research were designed to probe into this period of transition. Included below from the miscellaneous sample are typical responses from a 61-year-old mother of four; the mother was a daughter of missionaries to China:

Question: What was the transition like from your missionary community to work, junior college, Bible college, college, or university?

Mrs. Bain: I left the missionary school at about thirteen and lived with my mother and brother on Grandpa's farm. The community and public school was vastly different, and I always felt I was being treated like an oddity or freak. When I left there, I did not tell anyone of my background in hopes of being looked at as normal. I usually succeeded until I tried to explain my accent. Saying I had gone to an English [British] school sufficed usually. I still try to hide my beginnings and only tell about it when the truth is to my advantage.

Question: How did being a missionary son or daughter prepare you for
the world beyond the missionary environment?

> Mrs. Bain: It did not in any way. I actually left the missionary world at
> thirteen. But my mother did her best to preserve the world, and I feel now I
> would have only been fit for a convent. Her greatest disappointment was
> that I did not go out as a missionary.

Question: Did you sense a different approach to problems when you
compared yourself to your peers? If so, explain.

> Mrs. Bain: All through school, I felt as if I were groping for what [my
> peers] already knew in dealing with life. At church, I was at ease and often
> felt superior.

To summarize, often those making the transition out of the missionary
environment were in need of a catalyst. This was a common theme among
both the children of the Basel Mission's Children's Home [*Kinderhaus*]
and other samples. Various versions of the "catalyst" were given, including
the following:

Frau Spengler: When an inhabitant of the Basel Mission's *Kinderhaus*
turned sixteen, she or he had to leave. Frau Spengler described this exit as
"being thrown into cold water, although I was not so distressed as others."
She lived with a Basel family and helped in their home; then she lived
with a family in Heidelberg where she cared for infants. Life with the
Basel family was her catalyst to transition to a broader world. This
transition included a broader social concern and an awareness of her
responsibility to others.

Frau Roemer: Descending from generations of missionaries, Frau
Roemer lived in the *Kinderhaus* from age eight to fourteen. She felt that if
she had stayed longer, as some did during the war years, her development
would have been different. At fourteen, she was reunited with her family,
and the transition was not easy. Her own mother literally had not
recognized her when the mother returned from the mission field to Basel.
The mother could not see her as a "young woman." She and her mother
both had a hard time getting adjusted to each other again. The family
moved to Germany, and the relationships became easier and more routine.
Frau Roemer delighted in the freedom she had, especially the freedom to
develop her interests:

> Then I began to develop interests. That was something that was lacking in
> the Children's Home. One had only a little cultural stimulation or freedom
> of movement. One remained somehow small and modest!.... [Yet] we

wanted to be like others! For example, in [public] school, we didn't want to
be just the 'plain missionary children.'

Even though she felt different, Frau Roemer thought it advantageous
that she had been in a public school. This gave her a needed exposure to
other children, even though she and the other Children's Home inhabitants
were perceived as distinct. "One wasn't so secluded in the [public school],
and yet we were always depicted as *missionary children*." Even some of
the teachers discriminated against them with admonitions: "So, you want
to be missionary children, and you are so impudent." Frau Roemer just
wanted to be brave. Another chiding comment she heard was, "That must
not happen to missionary children!" Again, this was hard for her to bear,
because it made her feel so different.

Therefore, while she was 14 to 21, away from the Children's Home,
she had a *belatedly* happy childhood. The enjoyable "school spirit" in
Germany, the fine teacher she experienced there, and her training as a
kindergarten teacher established "a childhood for me which I lived and
experienced with full delight, much more aware and more active than I
could have been in Basel. There one was really somewhat confined." Her
eyes were opened!

She trained to be a kindergarten teacher with the intention of returning
to the Basel Children's Home, as a few others had also planned, to
improve the situation there. First, she taught in Germany, then supervised a
kindergarten. Later she was the director of a home for disadvantaged
children. This last experience more than any other served as her catalyst
into a world of self-understanding. It was as director of this home for
"socially neglected children" that she really could fulfill herself. She
gained a vantage point on her own childhood and observed how difficult it
is to raise children without a parental home, how hard it is for them to
become socially adjusted. Out of her own experience, she was benevolent
to these children. She was successful in her role as director. She
concluded: "I fulfilled myself and was also able to work through certain
things imbedded in my life."

Unfortunately, Frau Roemer's elder sister did not have such a
successful transition to the world beyond that of the mission home. At the
time of the interview, the sister tried to perpetuate the life of the
missionary parents by sitting in her mother's familiar chair and by writing
at the mother's desk. Referring to her parents, the elder sister insists: "In
this way, I must carry on." She lacked the catalyst to initiate her transition
into a life beyond that of her parents' milieu and into a life of her own.

Frau Walti, Frau Nill

For several of the married women who had lived as young girls in the Children's Home, their husbands served as a catalyst to the world beyond the Home. One interviewee remarked: "My husband gave me and showed me so much that I became a little bit freer. I was probably not so fully developed or mature when I left the Children's Home….A person receives perhaps a narrower perspective [in a children's home], and I had to work through all this in my later years. My husband helped me a lot with this."

Another former inhabitant of the Children's Home, at the time of the interview in her late fifties with grown children, echoed this sentiment. In particular, she credited her husband's help with her inhibitions and feelings of inferiority. She saw aspects of her inferiority complex in direct relation to the hierarchy established by the mission itself. She and others used the term "second class" to describe their relationship to the director's children and other children of the Basel Mission personnel living on the mission compound.

An interview with Frau Nill revealed more specifically the role of her husband as catalyst as she overcame self-doubt. She had always seen herself as an "onlooker" [*Anhaengsli*]. She also talked about the social hierarchy within the Children's Home as the director's children were treated as "first class." She and other children whose parents were away were "arranged at the lowest end of the [social ladder]." She still had this perception when she married. "I always thought: I belong in essence at the tail end of humanity. I was also shy about saying something in public."

Her husband, a psychiatrist by profession, encouraged her to extend herself in new ways. When she protested, he would say: "Try it once."

> I would say, 'I can't. I am a child from the Children's Home.' It was really almost in the sense of being a 'prisoner' or something like that, really feeling at the bottom end of humanity. This is the way people felt when they came out of the Children's Home. That could have been different through a little bit more integration. I believe that all of us had to overcome inhibitions with each other that are connected to our having inferiority complexes in every area. There were many who could not overcome them, even when they received help from their parents.

Frau Nill at age 18 had received help from her parents when they returned from the mission field. Her professional training served as an additional catalyst as she overcame inhibitions.

Other inhabitants of the Children's Home were not so fortunate. Many felt a distance between themselves and their returning parents. Remarks such as "I didn't know my mother" pertained to more than the initial reunion at the train station. For some, the natural contact with the mother (and father) was permanently lost. The difficulty of conforming to family life was often most severe for those who had spent the bulk of their puberty and adolescence in the Children's Home.

Not all interviewees were so fortunate to have catalysts. Among those who did, other variations of catalyst included professors such as Eduard Thurneysen or Karl Barth, teachers, training programs, non-missionary roommates, and other missionary children like themselves who had successfully made the transition to a wider world. This chapter has focused on interviews with former Swiss or German inhabitants of the Basel Children's Home located in Switzerland. Their transition from an enclosed mission compound [a hybrid culture] occurred within the European framework. However, children and adolescents from my other samples who had to move from one nation to another were confronted with a more extreme transition, compounded by the transnational nature of the move.

CHAPTER FIVE

TERRA FIRMA

Theological Import

Every person wants to belong. In psychological, sociological, and theological literature, there has been a shift from focus on the solitary self to the concept of a person as a self-in-relation.[1]

The actual cases I cite in this book beg the questions: Who am I? Where are my roots? Whose am I? Where do I belong? How do I belong? These questions are universals and happen to take us to the roots of theology.

In my research which spans over three decades, I have become increasing sensitive to the word "home." We often ask: Where is home? Statistics compiled in the United States on both the frequency of domestic abuse and of rape reveal that "home" is often a dangerous place. With one exception, I did not hear any narratives of parental or caretaker abuse in the 135 individuals interviewed for this book. The one exception was a resident of the Basel Mission Children's Home, a man whom I interviewed as an adult. When his missionary parents left for Ghana and left him at age 3 in the care of dorm parents in the Children's Home, he was understandably anxious. He wet his bed during the night. As a cure for this "condition," he had to stand in his wet underwear in the cold attic of the dorm. He developed a stutter in his speech at this stage of his development. When I interviewed him as an adult, he began to stutter as he told this memory.

Unfortunately, in my denomination, recent findings published in 2010 by the General Assembly Council of the Presbyterian Church USA have exposed physical and sexual abuse of children by Presbyterian missionaries in the Democratic Republic of Congo (Zaire, Belgian Congo)

---

[1] The Stone Center for Developmental Sciences and Studies at Wellesley College, Massachusetts, was the source for many manuscripts developing this concept: *self-in-relation*. In the 1980s, the work of Jean Baker Miller and Janet L Surrey advanced this concept at The Stone Center.

in the period 1945-1978.[2] The late Rev. William Pruitt was named as the chief perpetrator of sexual abuse in this report. I mention this report as an example of evidence that "home" may not be a place of firm footing or "solid ground" even when "home" is a mission boarding school. Therefore, I have chosen the term *terra firma* out of sensitivity to these findings.

This book is a work of historical theology with ramifications for a post-colonial theological anthropology. It augments an understanding of non-violent embodiment that has its foundation in incarnation. The reality of being born in a certain place and time, with sensory clues of belonging, imprinted with the gaze, the gleam, and the face of the beloved "other," is not one second removed from the experience of God becoming flesh in the "scandal of the particular." No amount of cell phones, Facebook, iPads, or LinkedIn Network can take away the primal significance of early space and initial bonding. Attachment theorists stress the importance of secure personal interactions and the dangers inherent in ruptures of relationships. Alfred Adler is one example of a theorist who maintained: every child has an inborn and innate need to belong and to connect with others.[3] Some recent theorists argue that technological advances can reduce personal interactions necessary for this "essential relatedness." This viewpoint will be a debate of the future. Regardless of the outcome of this debate, I would assert: One does not go "home" to Twitter. MIT (Massachusetts Institute of Technology) technology and society professor Sherry Turkle affirms this view. As a psychoanalytically trained psychologist, she argues that digital technology provides "substitutes" for connecting with others face-to-face.[4] "The new technologies allow us to 'dial down' human contact, to titrate its nature and extent."[5]

The bicultural "children" I have interviewed in their adult years do in fact stay in touch through e-mails, and when possible, through physical reunions. The electronic innovations like Facebook intensify the roots they formed earlier in a culture outside their country of citizenship and allow their *portable roots* and tendrils to touch familiar and firm ground.

---

[2] There is a 173-page report available for public reading issued by the Independent Commission of Inquiry Final Report (#5171002001) at http://www.pcusa.org/resource/final-report.

[3] Rachel Shifron, "Adler's Need to Belong as the Key for Mental Health," *The Journal of Individual Psychology*, Vol.66, No.1, Spring 2010, (Austin: University of Texas Press), pp.10-29.

[4] Sherry Turkle, *Alone Together: Why We Expect More From Technology and Less from Each Other* (New York: Basic Books, 2011), p. 11.

[5] Ibid, p. 15.

My research, in a way, documents nothing new. The Hebrew people as far back as Abraham, the wandering Aramean, wondered who they were, desiring roots in a longed-for land, migrating as an exodus people into new spaces, experiencing exile and root-lessness for much of their history, even as many Jewish people continue to experience *diaspora* today.

This chapter highlights older adults, some in their eighties and nineties, who have found a way to put their "portable roots" in *Terra Firma* or firm ground. These generative and seasoned adults offer their creative ways of *cultural consolidation*. All of them had USA citizenship at birth due to one or both parents. All but two were born in a second culture, i.e., a culture other than that of their citizenship (first culture). The two exceptions are Nicholas Van Dyck, born in California, but taken to China at three weeks of age, and Pearl Buck, born in West Virginia, but taken to China at three months of age. Six of them gave me interviews while I was a Resident Member at the Center of Theological Inquiry, Princeton. Each followed a set of fourteen questions that were identical to the questions asked of all my research samples. All of these individuals are persons in the generativity of their senior years; as such, they offer examples and insights of creative and successful integration of bicultural roots.

Pearl Buck and John Hersey, both deceased, left many writings from which I draw. In addition, there are biographies, and in Pearl Buck's case, an autobiography.

Ruth Carson West, born in Hong Kong;

Mary Davis, born in Nodoa on the island of Hainan [China];

Pearl S. Buck, born in Hillsboro, West Virginia; at three months of age, went with parents to Chinkiang, Shanghai, Nanhsuchou, Nanking [China];

John Hersey, born in Tientsin, China;

Nicholas Van Dyck, born in Pasadena, CA; at three weeks of age, went with parents to Anhui Province [China];

Tony Glockler, born in Beirut,Lebanon;

William Stoltzfus, born in Beirut, Lebanon.

Ruth Carson West: The Art of Resiliency

Ruth Carson West entered the world in a British hospital in Hong Kong in September of 1922. Her parents, North American agricultural and educational missionaries, were first stationed in Canton (Kwangchow), China, and worked in a secondary school. Ruth's father had been trained in rural sociology, and her mother was a teacher.

After Ruth was born, her mother developed a hearing problem. For medical and climate reasons, the family was advised to move to north China, to Shandong [Shantung], to a small missionary station where her brother Robert was born. At this time in China's history, Sun Yat-sen and Chiang Kai-shek were in power; the missionaries were welcomed. Thus, as a child, Ruth lived with her parents on the Cheeloo University campus in Shandong, China, where British, Canadian, and American missionaries worked together; they built a Christian university with "constructive cooperation." This cooperation was Ruth's early grounding in the links between ecumenicity and mission. According to Alison Gopnik, a psychology professor at The University of California, Berkeley, and a researcher in the study of empathy: "What studies show is that even extremely young babies can already understand something about what's going on in the minds of other people and can even to some extent take the perspective of other people."[6]

Ruth's brother was born when Ruth was two. When a major financial depression curtailed active missionary work, the family returned to the States where they based themselves in New York City. Ruth's father spent his time at Cornell University completing a doctorate in Rural Sociology. This subsequently prepared him to assume a post on the faculty at a newly constructed university in Tsinan (Jinan), Shandong, a first step in ecumenical outreach in mission. Ruth was sent to a private school, the Friends Academy, "to lighten the shock of being in a completely different culture." During this first furlough, the Depression started, and money dried up for the missionaries. They were delayed in the USA [1926-1932]. After returning to China, her sister Jean was born with Turners' Syndrome. Ruth was ten and remembers her mother's deep depression. This late child, her sister, "was a child of hope after they went back to the mission field." Her sister was lethargic, prone to infections, and passive. Ruth's mother's energy was directed toward the younger sister. Ruth was in a school run with largely British teachers. She began to get in trouble in school, something she had never done. The British teachers with kindness

---

[6] Sumathi Reddy, "Wise Beyond Their Years: What Babies Really Know," *Wall Street Journal*, February 12, 2013, D1.

spoke to her parents. A young American missionary wife, trained in managing girls' clubs, came to the campus and created activities for the girls. Ruth remembers with awe the generosity of adults who formed a community around the children like herself. At age eleven, Ruth was sent to boarding school at T'ungchow, a school just outside of Beijing. There she established friendships that have continued to the present day.

In 1937, when Ruth was in her freshman year of high school, the Japanese army arrived near her family's home on the east coast of China. There was killing in Shanghai and Nanking. Betty and John Stam in Tsingteh, China, were killed in 1934.[7] Ruth's family was never put in prison in China, although some of their friends were incarcerated after the communists seized control. Ruth summarizes this experience: "My parents were amazingly gracious people. They could have worked with almost anybody. We [the mission] had missionaries in Japan. It's the external structure of a country at war that breaks into that world where you can live peacefully with people. As a missionary, you don't ever feel hatred of the people attacking you, because you could have been missionaries there if the country had been different."

The Japanese invasion made it dangerous for her to return to boarding school. Some families chose to teach their children at home, but Ruth's family graciously accepted the generous offer of American Catholic sisters to provide education. Ruth was deeply impressed by the nuns who handled questions of faith with care; they had promised the missionary parents that they would not proselytize.

In 1938, Ruth's family was eligible for a second furlough. During this furlough, Ruth's father was asked to be President of Silliman [College] University which had been founded in 1901 by the Presbyterian Board of Foreign Missions at Dumaguete, Philippines. The goal of Silliman was to teach specific Christian values as a prerequisite to independence. As the Japanese army swept through China, Filipino faculty urged the pre-war faculty to guide them in achieving this goal. In 1939, two years away from high school graduation, Ruth arrived at Silliman with her family. Ruth describes this entry as "enveloped in the warmth and generosity of the Filipino staff, faculty, and students" in a way that she had never before experienced. In May 1942, the Japanese occupied the campus of Silliman University; many members of the Silliman faculty as well as the students were forced to evacuate the buildings and relocate to four localities. Under the leadership of Dr. Arthur Carson, Ruth's father, the operations of Silliman University continued in the mountains of Negros Oriental as a

---

[7] The Stams were missionaries with China Inland Mission and were attacked by bandits, The Red Army 19th Division.

"jungle university" for three years. By this time, Ruth was in the States for college. For two years, she did not know if her family was alive. Her brother had joined the guerillas in the Philippines. They all survived.

Ruth attended a community college in Missouri and later completed a degree at Barnard College; she went on for a masters and a doctorate in special education. In the interview, Ruth commented on all the supportive communities whether former missionaries, churches, or the Board of Foreign Missions that surrounded her years in the States. One Protestant chaplain and his family took her in as a "mother's helper." In this home, Ruth met her future husband, became engaged, and eventually greeted her family, smuggled out of the Philippines on an American submarine.

Ruth and her husband, Charles West, returned to China. When Ruth had to evacuate China with her small son to teach in post-war Silliman, she returned to many of her same Filipino friends. She taught special education at Silliman University. She gave workshops in Malaysia, Singapore, and Bangalore. She later taught autistic children in Princeton, New Jersey. While her husband taught at Princeton Theological Seminary, Ruth raised three sons, taught in a state hospital and later at university level. Her measure of success was as follows: "You need to show a person [who is] cut off from the culture a plausible, positive way into the culture itself. I learned this in special education." She also learned this as an infant in interaction with her environment.

In her autobiography, *Bend, Not Break*, Ping Fu discloses "the art of resiliency."[8] She talks about her childhood in China, her first culture. She describes the first eight years of her life as tranquil and happy. She attributes these early years or her first human perceptions as the foundation of her resiliency. The Taoist teachings of her Shanghai Papa centered around the flexibility of the bamboo trees in the garden. The bamboo bends but does not break! At age eight, Ping Fu was forcibly removed from the loving arms of her family members, branded as a "black element" in Mao Zedong's Cultural Revolution (1966-1976), put on a train to Nanjing, housed in a dormitory, forced to work long hours in a factory, and gang-raped. After committing a "political crime," she was expelled from China and immigrated to the USA. She is now chief executive for Geomagic. *Bend, not Break* reveals the tortuous odyssey of a Chinese woman who settles in the USA, her second culture. There are obvious differences in the journeys of Ping Fu and Ruth Carson West, both born in China. However, the commonality of their resilience cannot be missed.

---

[8] Ping Fu with MeiMei Fox, *Bend, Not Break: A Life in Two Worlds* (New York: Portfolio Penguin, 2012).

They are like two bamboos trees in the family gardens, trees well-rooted. Trees that bend, but do not break.

Mary McClintock Davis: The First Human Perceptions

Perhaps the first human perceptions stamped by life upon a newborn child were the ones which finally seemed most real. He and Mary had been born in China but Louise was American born....The first instincts of [Louise Liang's] flesh had entwined themselves with blue eyes and blond hair and white skin. (Pearl Buck)[9]

The theme of rootedness, belonging, and exile run through Buck's novel, *Kinfolk*. Dr. Liang, a scholar and an expert on Confucianism, lives in NYC, remote from his Chinese ancestors. He and his wife had an arranged Chinese marriage before they migrated to NYC with two young children, James and Mary. Later two more children (Louise and Peter) are born in the USA. At the end of the novel, the two older children (James and Mary) return to the ancestral village to settle and live with landlord Uncle Tao. In Pearl Buck's novel, Louise Liang assimilates into the country of her birth [USA] and marries a man with blue eyes, blond hair, and white skin.

Unlike the fictional Louise, Mary McClintock Davis had the opposite experience: Mary was born to North American parents in China. Like Louise, Mary was imprinted by her first human perceptions.

On Jan.27[th,] 1911, Mary McClintock Davis entered the world on the island of Hainan in the city of Nodoa. Her PCUSA missionary parents were with the Hainan Mission. They spent a year in Hoihow studying the Chinese language before they settled in Nodoa in the foothills region of Hainan, China. Hainan is an island south of mainland China. Brigands lived in the mountainous interior.

In an interview, Mary had vivid recollections from the time she was 2 and 3. Some of these involved sensory impressions, some were imprinted with emotions like fear of brigands or the loss of her brother, some were stamped with the need to belong: as a daughter, as a sister, as a playmate.

My first memories of China.... are of a big expanse of yard and lawn with all kinds of tropical trees – banana trees and pineapple-coconuts – bushes. [Our compound] had a big fence all around it. The warning from my father was: 'never, never can you go out that door'....that entrance to the compound. I had a nurse with me (an *Amah*); she was supposed to watch me all the time, but one day, however, I ran out the gate. I ran right square

---

[9] Pearl Buck, *Kinfolk* (New York: John Day Co., 1948), p.248.

into my father who was coming in…. He looked at me with amazement. He was so terrified. There were bandits in the mountains, bandits who picked up children, picked up animals, all to take back to their places in the mountains where they lived. That was really my first recollection...

Her older brother left for America when he was 14. He left [his pet] monkey with her. Mary was sad that she could never get the monkey to sleep with her as the monkey had done with her brother.

I remember seeing my brother getting on the boat. I guess he hugged my mother, father and me, but he held on to that monkey trying to take the monkey with him. Of course he couldn't, that is a very vivid memory – seeing him on that boat, seeing him leave….and leaving the monkey. [Mary was 6.]

Her brother never came back to China. He never saw his pet monkey again. Witnessing this departure of her older brother was an early perception of loss for Mary. Mary held on to the culture she knew in China as firmly as she wanted to hold the monkey.

Mary had a playmate who was Chinese. She spoke Chinese all the time. It was natural for Mary. It was not natural to be put on exhibit or "on display" when she returned for furlough to the USA.

I have the memories of a little Chinese playmate. I talked Chinese all the time. My parents talked English to me which I understood. Once I visited my aunt in Portland, Oregon; I was 5-7 years old. My aunt had a party for my mother. Someone wanted me to speak Chinese. My mother asked me a question in Chinese. I said: 'I'll never speak Chinese again!' They coaxed me with dolls and toys, but I never did!

Her connections to her life in China were precious ones. Her mother's critical illness caused anxiety: connections can be broken. They are precarious. Her mother was taken to Hong Kong. The doctors in Hong Kong could not make a diagnosis.

Every time a boat would land in Hong Kong, they would ask the ship doctors to look at her. One day a boat from Africa landed, and they asked the doctor to see my mother. He went to the hospital…the minute he walked in the room, he said: 'I know what she has.' They said: 'What do you mean, you haven't even examined her?' He said: 'She has a liver abscess, and I can tell by the odor.' He was from Africa. He was very prominent in Africa. He had the right medicine for it. She was cured.

My father had taken me every day to the hospital to see my mother. I didn't want to go. I said: 'That's not my mother.' I had never seen my mother still and quiet. So this day, when the doctor came in, I saw her, and she was sitting up in a wheelchair, and I said: 'My mother has come back.' I ran to my father, and I said: 'Here is my mother. I told you that wasn't my mother. Here she is.' She was sitting in a wheelchair. That was a BIG moment. I remember walking every day up that hill in Hong Kong.

When Mary came to the USA, she lived with her grandmother in Los Angeles, California. Her mother went all over the country talking about missions for the Foreign Mission Board (PCUSA northern branch). Mary's father suffered what was at the time labeled "a nervous breakdown" and was placed in a hospital for recuperation.

They later lived together as a family in Colorado Springs. Both brothers went to college, one at the University of Alabama and the other at the University of Minnesota. Her father couldn't take the altitude in Colorado so Mary and her parents went to Laurel, Mississippi. This is where Mary witnessed her mother being reprimanded for speaking to African-Americans as equals.

Mary recounts the true story of Leontyne Price [American soprano] who came from Laurel, MS. "She had such a beautiful voice. She sang in the Metropolitan. They wouldn't let her sing in the high school in Laurel; she had to sing in her church in Laurel."

In Laurel, MS, a churchwoman told my mother how to address African-Americans: "They're different. You don't talk to them like you talk to someone who is brought up like you are." My mother couldn't understand that. My mother addressed a woman who was African-American as Mrs. Smith. The Laurel church woman said: "You never call them by the name *Mrs.*" My mother said: "Why not? Isn't she married?"

My idea of the world was different, especially being in Laurel, Mississippi, with so many African-Americans. I didn't understand why there was any difference. I feel that everybody is the same, I don't care what the skin color. That was born into me. My parents never spoke of people being different because they were Chinese or Japanese or African. It didn't make any difference. You were somebody that God loved. That was taught to me from an early age. There were no racial prejudices. God loved everyone. You don't go in to missions if you don't feel that. You give up your life for that.

Yes, I have had a very different outlook because of my parents and their view of life. I still feel that same way. God loves us all. I still feel that same way....Maybe you need to be born into it somehow.

Mary Davis was 101 years old at the time of the interview. She is now 103 and filled with a wisdom that began with her "first human perceptions." I was a teacher at St. Mary's Episcopal School in Memphis, Tennessee, when she was Dean in the early 1970s. She courageously stood with Head of School Nat Hughes to allow persons of all colors to be admitted. St. Mary's was the first private school in Memphis to do so; the action was before the Supreme Court's ruling. A Board of Trustees member resigned, parents transferred children out of the school, but Mary Davis stood firm in her "first human perceptions." Her tenacity of spirit had allowed her to survive as a young widow of three girls many years earlier. She concluded our interview with the observation: "It is a lovely day. The sky is blue." I was told to adjourn, go outside, and seize the day. I obeyed.

Pearl S. Buck: The White Roses

"Double worlds" exist for those bicultural children like the writer and philanthropist Pearl Sydenstricker Buck (Sai Zhenzhu). Pearl Buck lived 42 years in China, 39 years in the USA. Her novels such as the *The Good Earth*, *Sons*, and *A House Divided* testify to her intimacy with China. Again, cultural intimacy is deep understanding and close association with a physical place, region of a country, or a nation. Pearl Buck had her feet planted firmly in two worlds.

This was not the case for her mother, Carie, about whom Pearl wrote in *The Exile*. Carie had left the USA as a young and idealistic bride, hoping that God would speak to her on the mission field. God did not. God was especially silent when Carie buried three of her children in the soil of China. Carie remained rooted to the USA, but became bound to China.

> Gradually it came to her that rooted as she was by birth and love to this country of her own, to America, yet she was also bound to China, bound by her very knowledge of it, bound by such souls as Wang Amah, bound by the three small bodies sleeping in that ancient earth and mingling at last their pale dust with its darkness. Ah, that country was no longer alien to her now. She could bear to go back one day, because some of her own flesh and spirit lay buried there.[10]

The eldest child, Edwin, survived. After the loss of two children, Carie had Pearl whom she called Comfort. In sibling order, Pearl was fourth out of seven children. All of the children died with the exception of Edwin, Pearl, and Grace. Pearl remembers her mother's visit to the graves in

---

[10] Pearl Buck, *The Exile* (New York: John Day Co., 1936), p.172.

Shanghai and the significance of the planting of the root of a white rose tree.

> .... there she planted the root of a white rose tree that she had brought from the porch of her home [in West Virginia]. On the day of her departure she had dug it up and wrapped it well in earth and moss and sacking, and had watered it all the way across the sea. 'These little three never saw our America, their own land,' she said to Edwin sorrowfully as he helped her. 'They were born and died in an alien country and it will make me happier to think there is something of America and of our own home above them for beauty and a covering.'[11]

The white rose grew and thrived. In a later memory, Pearl Buck described her mother in the courtyard in Tsingkiangpu with white roses in one hand and Edwin in the other.

Carie befriended a destitute Chinese woman who became widowed with a ten-year-old daughter, Precious Cloud. When the widow became gravely ill, Carie offered to raise Precious Cloud as a daughter. As the widow died, she asked Carie: "Why have you loved me, who am not of your blood and bone?" Carie: "I do not know except that the need of your heart has pulled my heart and we are the children of one Father, after all."[12]

When the time came for Edwin and Pearl to settle in the USA for college, Carie said farewell to the USA forever. She brought America to the expatriates in China, especially the USA naval personnel stationed nearby. Carie invited them for home-cooked meals in her home in Tsingkiangpu, which she had fixed up to look a little American. Carie "had learned now that home and country are in one's own heart, and may be created according to the heart's desire anywhere in the world."[13] According to Pearl Buck, "....now she [Carie] turned her face toward the exile and steadily she turned, for all of America now, her America, was in her heart and in her memories."[14]

Pearl Buck spent most of the first forty years of her life in China where she did feel rooted. In 1934, because of conditions in China, and to be closer to Richard Walsh and her daughter Carol, Buck moved permanently to the USA. Carol had been born with PKU (phenylketonuria) and needed medical care. Pearl Buck and her second husband (Richard Walsh) founded Welcome House, the first international, inter-racial adoption

---

[11] Ibid., p.179.
[12] Ibid., p.213.
[13] Ibid., p.260.
[14] Ibid., p.271.

agency. Buck became an advocate for special needs, transracial, and international adoption. For Amerasian children who were considered "unadoptable," Buck established the Pearl S. Buck Foundation to sponsor funding for literally thousands of children. By mid-life, she and Richard had adopted seven children, four of whom were biracial.

Buck's life is one portrayal of "bringing two worlds together," of *cultural consolidation*, of standing with both feet on *terra firma*. As I sat by Pearl Buck's grave in the Spring of 2012 at Green Hills Farm, Perkasie, Pennsylvania, there were flowers, shrubs, trees rooted all around her grave. Her testament to her two worlds faced me: an American grave with her Chinese name in characters inscribed on the grave marker: Sai Zhenzhu.

John Hersey:
"My mother's mother must have been like her"

John Richard Hersey (1914-1993) was the child of USA missionaries to China. Hersey was born in Tientsin, China, and learned to speak Chinese before English. He lived in China until age ten when his parents returned to the USA. John wrote about his "absentee father" and his sacrificial mother in the historical novel, *The Call* (1985). This novel is one of many examples of Hersey's style: a bridging of storytelling (novel) with non-fiction reporting. In this historical novel, through many religious maneuvers, his father Roscoe Hersey loses his "call" from God. He has also lost the chance to know his sons well and severed the emotional connection with his longsuffering and saintly wife, Grace Baird Hersey. It must be said that Roscoe Hersey loved China above all else, even his family.

John Hersey was a bicultural child, spending birth to ten years of age in what was his "second culture." Upon return to his first culture or place of citizenship, John Hersey began to display remarkable talents in journalism and reporting. It was his bicultural sensitivity and bicultural identity which allowed him to be a cultural interlocutor.

As an example, in the Pulitzer Prize-winning novel, *A Bell for Adano*,[15] Hersey endowed his protagonist, bicultural Major Victor Joppolo, with the role of go-between or translator. Major Joppolo, U.S.A., was the Amgot (Allied Military Government Occupied Territory) officer of a small Italian town called ADANO. Major Joppolo, called "Mister Major" by the townspeople, was an Italian-American assigned to work in Italy. He spoke

---

[15] John Richard Hersey, *A Bell for Adano* (New York: Alfred A. Knopf, 1944).

fluent Italian because his parents were from Florence. He had the dark skin of his parents. Upon arriving in Adano, Major said to Official Borth: "'....this is like coming home, how often have I dreamed this.' And he bent over, and touched the palm of his hand to the jetty, then dusted his palm off on his woolen pants."[16]

The town of Adano had been crippled with bombs. Grey dust, bomb craters, shell holes were everywhere. The people were in hiding.

> At the corner of the third alley running off the Via of October Twenty-eight, the two men came on a dead Italian woman. She had been dressed in black. Her right leg was blown off and the flies for some reason preferred the dark sticky pool of blood and dust to her stump. 'Awful,' the Major said, for although the blood was not yet dry, nevertheless there was already a beginning of a sweet but vomitous odor. 'It's a hell of a note,' he said, 'that we had to do that to our friends.' 'Friends,' said Borth, 'that's a laugh.' 'It wasn't them, not the ones like her,' the Major said. 'They weren't our enemies. My mother's mother must have been like her. It wasn't the poor ones like her; it was the bunch up where we're going, those crooks in the City Hall.'[17]

Throughout the novel, Major Joppolo showed a willingness to listen and even identify with the townspeople. They grew to trust – even love him. They had a portrait made of him and a celebration even as he received orders to leave Adano. For him, the restored bell of Adano tolled!

Hersey continued in his work as cultural interlocutor in WWII as he traveled as war correspondent in Europe and Asia and wrote for *Time* and *Life*. Hersey accompanied the Allied troops. Following the lead of a Jesuit priest in Japan, Hersey reported from Hiroshima and interviewed survivors of the bombing of Hiroshima. Again, he combined narrative with history in the 31,000 word article "Hiroshima" for *The New Yorker* (1946). At one point, *Time* sent him to the Chongqing bureau. Hersey wrote about the Warsaw Ghetto in *The Wall* as he continued his work in civil rights and anti-war efforts.

In *The Call,* as he described the generation of missionaries to China in the early 1900s, he mentioned the phenomenon of "expatriation sickness." This term was used of a USA Lutheran missionary who had to return to the USA under orders to evacuate in war. This missionary suffered "expatriation sickness" on the vessel to the USA, died, and was buried at sea. The longing of the expatriate was for China, not the first culture

---

[16] Ibid., p.3.
[17] Ibid., pp.5-6.

[USA]. As a bicultural child, Hersey saw this, knew this, exposed this in his literary fashion. It takes a cultural interlocutor to convey: "My mother's mother must have been like her!"

As we examine the lives of Ruth Carson West, Mary Davis, Pearl Buck, and John Hersey, the impact of cultural cues when they were babies is evident. Scientists at the Institute for Learning and Brain Sciences, at the University of Washington in Seattle, use MEG (magnetoencephalography) or brain imaging on babies to measure magnetic-field changes on the brain. Early cues and interactions have been shown to have a profound impact on brain development. By age 1, a child's brain volume is 70% of an adult's, 85% by three years of age. As new technology enables researchers to understand how a baby's brain interacts with its environment, more insight will accrue on the imprint of the early years on the brain of the bicultural child.

Nicholas Van Dyck, Tony Glockler, William Stoltzfus: Bamboo shoots

Waiting for the imminent birth of his younger brother, the innocent Yul-chun in his childish anger destroyed several of the young shoots in the bamboo grove of the family's garden. Several hundreds of the young shoots, ivory in casings of green, were above ground. Some tens were broken off and destroyed by the young child. Il-han, his father, said with sadness: "The plants these shoots might have been, waving their delicate leaves in the winds of summer, will never live....Though it is only a hollow reed, it is a living reed. Now the roots must send up other shoots to take the place of those you have destroyed. Do you understand me?"[18]

....in our country [Korea] the bamboo shoot is the symbol of the strong uprising spirit of a [person]. Perhaps the [person] is a great poet, or an artist, or perhaps he is a leader among the people, even a revolutionist. It is easy to crush these bamboo shoots....It is easy to destroy but hard to create. Remember that when you want to destroy something.[19]

Nicholas Van Dyck

Nicholas, born in Pasadena, California, was three weeks of age when his parents took him to Anhui Province in inland China. Nicholas' parents were PCUSA educational missionaries. Nicholas' mom was more present

---

[18] Pearl S. Buck, *The Living Reed* (New York: John Day Co., 1963), p.27.
[19] Ibid., p.159.

in his childhood because his father was often away evangelizing or saving souls.

Nicholas lived in a walled city which was 3,000 years old. "Everything always seemed to be right and natural, especially at home. I had a very best friend, a gateman's son, Bo Gwan Sun. He and I played together; we had a great time. We went into the forest of bamboo and hid. We climbed on the wall that surrounded the compound until one of the missionaries told us to get off lest we break our necks." From infancy to 7 years of age, Nicholas spoke Chinese with friends and English with his parents. With his *Ama*, Liu Dao Ma, who "lived out what it is to have a loving presence," he spoke Chinese.

Nicholas remembered the last time he saw his best friend, Bo Gwan Sun. Nicholas was 8, and Bo Gwan Sun was 12. They were in the compound in this rural province of China when the Japanese came. Bo Gwan Sun was put in a line-up. The Japanese took him away. Nicholas' family went to the USA for furlough and was prevented from returning due to the war. At age eleven, Nicholas studied Mandarin at the graduate school of Chinese Studies at Yale University in New Haven. When Nicholas and his family went back to China in 1945, Bo Gwan Sun was nowhere to be seen.

Nicholas went to school in Shanghai in 1945-46. In 1947-1948, the school was evacuated to Hangkow. In 1948-1949, he was moved to Hong Kong, then back to China until 1949. His 11th and 12th grades were spent in boarding school at The Stony Brook, fifty miles east of New York City with his parents nearby.

The evangelical Presbyterian college of Whitworth in Spokane, Washington, was not engaging enough so he left after two years. "I wasn't made for it." He was made for the Naval Air Corps and wanted to see the world. As a pilot, he was in a squadron where Jewish, Roman Catholic, and other faith traditions were represented. There [in the navy] he began to ask the questions: "How could this God let words flow from the mouth as remembered or reconstructed by an institutionally contaminated writer like the apostle Paul who was writing things that would keep the church going? Jesus never mentioned the church. Jesus talked about how behavior and actions would make a difference in the *eternal now*, the idea of waiting until later (for that kind of life) didn't make sense to Jesus or me. I have felt critical of the institution, to have a product: everyone has sinned so you need our product of forgiveness! [This is] manipulative and political. People think they know what is right for everyone in the world." His orientation became more progressive. The navy was where he questioned the exclusivism of Christianity. "My faith as an adult is radically different from that of my missionary child upbringing."

> One of the things in retrospect that began to gnaw on me, the kind of Christianity I had been exposed to so far, didn't include my little friends [Chinese friends] or a lot of people I saw. I didn't understand how a loving God couldn't save everybody in the world. It is my major argument with Christianity.

The adventurous Nicholas was in the navy from 1954-1958. Then he completed degrees at Union Seminary in NYC (M.Div.) and at The University of St. Andrews in Scotland (Ph.D.). He became a PCUSA pastor in Palisades, New York, married in 1958 (Marcia), and later taught at Princeton Theological Seminary.

Like a bamboo shoot, Nicholas has put down tendrils of tenacity and shown adaptability in his religious rootedness. He gave credit to many lessons learned from his parents. "My parents had a deep running respect for all the people around them; the Chinese people we were with commanded our utmost courtesy...." "We felt relatively at home in other cultures. We visited with them when we traveled; [we didn't stay] in the high hotels." His dad moved the family into a grass-roofed hut, out of the lovely house in the pompom. It was such a different life than for other missionaries. "He [dad] was before his time. I have picked up some of his ways."

Nicholas' mother gave him a sense of being cared for and protected. Japanese soldiers once slept in her flower garden; flowers were destroyed. Nonplussed she said, "Spring will come." Nicholas learned an adaptability that is not unlike the flexible spreading of young bamboo shoots.

There were painful memories as well, painful memories of the Sino-Japanese War. "Our mission compound was used with the hospital to take care of the dying. [I remember] the smell of the dying. My parents were giving people glasses of water to drink. I had occasional nightmares. We do terrible things to each other when we stop being peacemakers and concentrate on being warriors. I was sensitized to poverty and disease."

Nicholas has the freedom to question. "My concern is to get a firm understanding of the Resurrection apart from the magic. This is a difficult transition. Once you start talking like that, there are many lovingly faithful people who think I have rejected their fathers and the faith they held as a child." Nicholas talked often about childhood and adult faith. The roots of the latter have spread and flourished.

Tony Glockler

I was born [April 2, 1936] in Beirut, Lebanon, to a missionary couple. My father was an Englishman; he was born in Beirut also. His father came to Lebanon when the mission opened a printing press; my grandfather was a 'press man.' He came to help with the printing of Bibles, hymnals, etc. My mother's maiden name was Jessup. The Jessups came to Lebanon when Lincoln was President. My great-grandfather was Samuel Jessup, and his brother Henry Harris Jessup came to Lebanon in the late 1850s and 1860s and a Jessup returned to the field until my mother. That reflected about one hundred years of Jessup presence in the mission field in Lebanon.[20]

Both of Tony's parents, having been born in Lebanon, were fluent in Arabic and in French. Tony spoke as many words of Arabic as of English. Then he started attending a French school for kindergarten, first, second, and third grades and became trilingual. In fact the summer between third and fourth grade, he had to take English lessons from his grandfather because although he spoke it, he didn't write English. He wrote French.

Neither of his parents was ordained. His father went to the American University of Beirut after going to a German preparatory school; he studied business administration. Tony's father took over the printing business from Tony's grandfather and was ultimately promoted to Treasurer of the Lebanon/Syria Mission. He handled all of the business aspects of the mission field. Tony's mother was a teacher and principal of the ASG (American School for Girls) in Beirut, a school operated by the mission. Tony developed a spirit of hospitality towards other religions. He commented on the values in his family: "We grew up as a happy family. It didn't depend on money. It didn't depend on owning a lot of things…[like] automobiles. We understood the source of happiness is not the accumulation of wealth or the results of wealth. That is a big advantage."

He had a lot of positive influences on his faith. His family attended church each Sunday. "I don't mean this negatively but Christianity was taken for granted. My grandparents and parents were Christian missionaries. That is both a plus and a minus. For a child who is not yet old enough to ponder theology, it was a plus." Tony did not view his family as pious. In the interview, he gave an anecdote as illustration. "One Easter, there was an Arabic language service preceding the English

---

[20] Henry Harris (H.H.) Jessup wrote a long two volume memoir of his time in Lebanon: *Fifty-three Years in Syria* (New York: Fleming H. Revell Co., 1910), Vols. I and II. In pre-Ottoman times, there was no distinction between Lebanon and Syria. The volumes include a list of missionaries in the Syria Mission from 1819-1908. (Appendix, p.797) A theological seminary was opened in Beirut in 1873.

language service. My father was responsible for some of the setup of the English service that day. He was waiting outside for the Arabic language service to finish. They ran long. He was getting impatient. One of the Lebanese men ran out: 'Mr. Glockler! Mr. Glockler! Christ has risen!' My father said: 'It's about time!'"

Growing up in Lebanon in the 1940s, Tony was exposed to both Christians and Muslims. According to Tony, conversion was not a focus of his parents' mission in Lebanon, but supporting the local Protestant community.

Although Lebanon was majority Christian, and minority Muslim, the two religions interacted as two Abrahamic faiths in Tony's opinion. Tony still maintains contact with Samir, a regular playmate in Lebanon. Samir is now an M.D. in southern New Jersey

"I don't think of myself as very spiritual, yet I am faithful in attending church very regularly. [Tony then mentioned numerous committees on which he had served.] I am committed not just in intent but in fact to our church, but I don't think of myself as spiritual, pious."

In Tony's words, he has moved from a non-questioning stance towards Christianity to an inquiring one. His religious outlook is not the orthodox one of his youth. "I'm not sure that God exists in the orthodox sense of it. I think God is the most wonderful idea that humanity has ever come up with... [Humankind] needed an idea, and the idea got gradually refined; the life of Jesus Christ refined the idea to its highest and most perfect level. So I believe that is a level which is constantly setting a bar that I confess I fail to meet, but at least, it is worth the attempt."

Significant to his faith development was a marker event when his parents were away from Lebanon on furlough in 1947. In 1948, his family returned as Arabian oil fields were being discovered, and the "Tapline" was built through Lebanon. Suddenly, the student body at the American Community School changed as oil company executives sent their children to the school. Up to that point, the majority of students were children of missionaries or of employees/professors at the American University of Beirut (AUB). In 1948, these children became the minority. It became a boarding school with new slang, new songs, new dress. These were "foreigners" to Tony. They didn't speak Arabic, and they didn't have an interest in learning Arabic. "All of a sudden there was this other culture coming in...."

In the summer of 1951, Tony had to return to the USA for five years to establish his USA citizenship. He was registered on his mother's passport to travel, but his citizenship was conditional on being in the USA for five years before age 21. Tony's parents put him on a boat and said: "Have a nice trip." "When my daughter was 15, I thought, 'could I take her down to Port Newark and stick her on a boat?' No way! But, it was not a problem [for my parents]....When my back was turned, I am certain that my mother was going for the tissues as I am just thinking about it."

Tony was befriended by a young pastor's family on the boat. The daughter was about Tony's age and invited him to a dance. He did not have experience with dancing so he feigned illness. Tony felt so like "a fish out of water." This was just one example of his difficulty in acculturation.

Tony's uncle met him at the dock in the USA. His aunt and uncle were his substitute parents for 6 years (New Hampshire). "That eased the transition a whole lot because I had a safe haven." Tony boarded at Mount Hermon Boarding School in Massachusetts where he described his acculturation as somewhat difficult. Tony graduated and enrolled in Colby College where as a senior lab instructor in physics, he met Bev who later became his wife. Tony described dating as painful for him because he had no experience. He was painfully shy and didn't know how to go about asking for a date. It took some months before he asked her out. "I paid for the movie. She hadn't had dinner yet. She had a chocolate bar with her. I ended up eating her chocolate bar. That was her dinner!"

As is typical for those of multiple cultures, Tony wanted to return overseas. In 1957, when Tony graduated from Colby College, he hoped to go into the Diplomatic Corps. He passed the Foreign Service entrance exam on the first try. He was interviewed by three retired Foreign Service diplomats. Tony was barely 21. The Chair of the Exam Committee suggested Tony wait for three years due to his youth.

Tony kept looking for a job in the Middle East but he started moving up the ladder in an insurance agency. He was a computer programmer and loved his work. He was rapidly promoted to manager and stayed seven years. He was married in 1961. Meanwhile, Tony's brother did manage to travel as a Naval Lieutenant. Tony's parents had retired in Mercerville, NJ. Educational Testing Services (ETS) in Princeton, New Jersey, had an opening. Tony went for an interview and was hired. Every three years he got promoted until he retired in 2001. He and his wife, Bev, have been in the same house since 1965.

Tony was most successful in his career especially in the area of multi-tasking. "The fact that I was multi-lingual gives me mental flexibility more so than some....I could actually speak English to people so they understood what I was saying." Tony had to be "multilingual," using technical terms with technicians and business terms with clients. We discussed Tony's exposure to different types of music. Tony noticed that his accents (French and Arabic) don't deteriorate with age. Since 2001,

Tony has been a volunteer ambulance driver. Even in retirement, he continues to serve others. He concludes the interview:

> I suppose this links back to the missionary culture, the *raison d'être* ....missionaries being concerned about doing things for others without regard for the financial consequences. When I look back at the missionaries who were there in the late 1800s, there were brilliant people, scholars in Arabic, working at missionary wages. Who knows what their careers would have been in this country. My great-grandfather and grandfather were both Yale grads, working in the mission field. This is in my genes to try to do something to try to be helpful for other people.

William (Bill) Stoltzfus

"I consider Lebanon my home, when I think of home, I think of Lebanon." Bill Stoltzfus recounted first the roots his parents had put down in Lebanon, then his own roots.

Bill's father was a Mennonite from Ohio; his mother was a Presbyterian from Minnesota. Both went to Lebanon after WWI. Bill's mother taught in an orphanage in Sidon. His father took supplies to the various missions in Tripoli, Sidon, Beirut. Bill's father decided to join The Presbyterian Board of Foreign Missions. Bill's parents were sent to Nabatiya, a town in southern Lebanon, then Souq al-Gharb, then Aleppo in Syria for ten years, back to Beirut to the Lebanese American University until 1956. His father was an educator. The Lebanese American University library was dedicated to his late father in 2007, and Bill and family members were present for this dedication.

> I was born in Beirut, Lebanon (1924); I grew up there. We were in Lebanon a couple of years before we moved to Aleppo, Syria, where my father was principal of the North Syrian School for Boys for 10 years. Then he was transferred to Lebanese American University in Beirut; I went to school in the American Community School in Beirut until I was 15.

Bill came by ship to the USA for 11th and 12th grades at Deerfield Academy in Massachusetts. He spoke French, Arabic, and English. His transition to the States was a huge one. He didn't know how to mail a letter because he had not seen a mailbox. He was awkward meeting girls. "They found me a bit strange, but they were nice to me." "I was never homesick." "I enjoyed travelling and moving around."

"I missed my parents, but wasn't sad or depressed." Bill's father, a President of Beirut University, prepared him for the world outside the mission field. Bill's parents did not proselytize, nor did his father preach.

Bill did not grow up in a mission atmosphere, but a collegiate atmosphere. "There was no religious aspect to my growing up at all." They said grace at meals. "I never thought of my parents as missionaries." His mom said: "I came out to sacrifice and do good works. I have never sacrificed." Bill's parents were entwined in the community. They were into education and leading an exemplary life. "They had no intention of telling others what to do." "They never put any pressure on me."

Bill went to Princeton University for one year; afterwards, he joined the Naval Air Corps for two years as a pilot. Returning to Princeton, he then graduated in 1949 followed by admittance into the Foreign Service. "The Foreign Service was looking for non-ivy league types. After a training program for 9 months, I went to Benghazi, Libya (two years), then Alexandria, Egypt, then back to the States to take the Foreign Service Exam. I passed. Then I studied more Arabic in a language training program for the State Department in 1953. Then, I was appointed Vice Consul in Kuwait from 1954-1956. I went to Syria in 1956 during the Suez Crisis and was appointed Political Officer at the USA Embassy in Damascus (1956-1959). They [Department of State] didn't want me to get too *Arabized,* so I came to the Personnel Department in Washington (1961-1964), was an assistant to Everill Harriman (1965), and worked for the National War College (1966). Later, I was sent as Assistant to the USA Ambassador in Jidda, Saudi Arabia, for two years then to Ethiopia (1966-1968), then back to Saudi Arabia (1968-1971), then Kuwait (1972-1976), then to Yemen, Qatar, and Oman." Bill held distinguished positions during the later moves: he was appointed United States Ambassador to Kuwait, Bahrain, Qatar, the United Arab Emirates, and Oman. He left the Foreign Service in 1976 and went to a Financial Firm as "the Middle East man."

Bill reflected on his Christian upbringing. "My parents put no heat on me. I go to church now every Sunday because I know Janet [my wife] would want me to. I am definitely an agnostic although I do all the things you are supposed to do. I know the Apostle's Creed by heart although 90% of it, I don't believe."

Bill sees his advantage in living overseas, learning the language, loving the people. There was no question about what he wanted to do after college. "They [my parents] never put any pressure on me. I had no interest in missionary work. I knew I wanted to live abroad." "I'm 87 now. When I got to 85, I said: 'I've had a wonderful life. It doesn't matter a damn what happens after this.'" "Why wouldn't anyone be happy that everything worked out well?"

Nicholas Van Dyck, Tony Glockler, and William Stoltzfus all sent out tendrils throughout the world while remaining connected in *Terra Firma.*

Foreign Service, the navy, or the diplomatic corps are not uncommon
goals or choices for the bicultural child.

L'Enracinement: "Taking root"

A sixty-year-old European woman told me of her brother's agonizing
struggle to accept his life's fate as the son of missionaries and to resolve
the bitterness he felt towards family and mission. He had been left in
Europe at the age of one and a half when his parents went to Africa. He
bore a deep resentment toward his parents for leaving him in the Basel
Children's Home which meant that he eventually attended a German
school. He seldom joined his parents when they returned from the mission
field. He was outspoken against Christianity, the church, and "mission
patriots." In his retirement, he and his sister were invited to attend the
mission field where his parents, now deceased, had labored. His sister
recalled the impact this visit made upon him:

> My brother came back an entirely changed person... because he finally
> understood his parents. And it was really an overwhelming experience for
> him. ...I saw my brother change his whole attitude toward the mission,
> because, as he said, 'It never occurred to me that these missionaries ...were
> giving their lives so that these Africans could be liberated. We missionary
> children thought only, 'How can our parents live there?'

> Before he died, my brother and I discussed many things, and I think his
> faith was able to grow again. ...Two weeks before he died, he heard me
> preparing a talk for a feminist theology seminar. I asked him about Simone
> Weil, the French philosopher. He had just written about her and about her
> understanding of faith. Through her, he came to understand that Christ was
> something other than Christianity and the church.

> And he used a word of Simone Weil in her writings on uprooted people
> who are able to re-root. Weil wrote about deprived people, our secular
> people, in Europe and in America, people who have been deprived of their
> home country. Uprooted and then rerooted. Weil tried to show how these
> uprooted people could find new roots for their faith. My brother said to me,
> 'If you want to say something to these theologians about *l'enracinement*
> [taking root], don't tell them about Simone Weil. Tell them about Jesus
> Christ – He is the only one who can give us roots.' And two weeks later he
> died. I officiated at the funeral, and I shared these thoughts. There were
> official delegates there who didn't want to hear anything about faith! But I
> believe I made these officials think about my brother's path of reluctance
> and then of growing faith.

> That life is closed now.

But the lives of many more children continue to struggle with their parents' commitment to another homeland. These children, as they reach adolescence, will also be challenged to decide or discover who they are, where they belong, and to whom and to what they have allegiance.

CHAPTER SIX

ROOT SYSTEMS

Generalizability and Particularities

Recently, I presented my work on the bicultural child at a national convention. After the question and answer period, one woman remained behind and raised a challenging issue. This theological educator was in her forties; as an African-American, she had lived most of her early life as a minority in a dominant white culture. Her point was that she was a bicultural child as were other African-Americans. Their first culture would be that of various parts of Africa from whence their ancestors were forcibly uprooted.

Her perceptive comment caused me to rethink the generalizability and particularity of my usage of the term, bicultural child. I have used it to describe someone who has grown up in their early developmental years (birth/infancy to ages 18-21) in a physical, external system or space that functions as a primary culture. The core task of late teen years into early young adulthood is identity formation. This includes *cultural consolidation* which is rootedness in culture(s). This core task is a generalizable one for all young people. For those with "portable roots" which involve transplanting in a secondary culture, the complexity of this task has its particularities. The transplanting takes the child/adolescent through a liminal space, a threshold between two distinct cultures, which again marks the experience of the bicultural child as distinctive. The liminal threshold or interstitial borderland involves the physicality of space, land, climate, social networks, art, foods, geography, celebrations, rituals, and all forms of sensory reception.

"Portable roots" as a concept can be applied to transplanted children of immigrant, refugee, transnational, borderland, and other hybrid communities. The cultural equilibrium of bicultural children is often upset when they return to their "first culture" and struggle for identity or when they seek to blend into their "second culture." The process of re-organization raises the most profound questions of home, belonging, and rootedness. It begs the question of "who we are." Let it be said that the transplanted bicultural child who is able to consolidate his or her cultural identity emerges as a more capable world citizen, better equipped for interpersonal and intercultural intimacy, poised for generativity, and positioned for ego integrity and leadership. It is simply a more arduous task to get there.

Previous research has introduced terms such as *double consciousness* (Du Bois), spiritual refugees (Archie Smith), and relational refugees (Toni Morrison). W.E.B. Du Bois was a pioneer in the understanding of *double consciousness* as looking at one's self through the eyes of the dominant race:

> It is a peculiar sensation, this *double consciousness*, this sense of always looking at one's self through the eyes of others, of measuring one's soul by the tape of a world that looks on in amused contempt and pity. One ever feels his twoness, – an American, a Negro; two souls, two thoughts, two unreconciled strivings; two warring ideals in one dark body, whose dogged strength alone keeps it from being torn asunder.
>
> The history of the American Negro is the history of this strife – this longing to attain self-conscious manhood, to emerge his double self into a better and truer self.[1]

Archie Smith, Jr., used the concept "spiritual refugees" for those Africans who were uprooted from the ancestral land and brought through force to the shores of America as slaves and black fugitives. The spiritual refugee today shares these characteristics in being "uprooted, homeless, and landless; seeking shelter in another place; losing the protection of one's rights; imprisonment; and deportation."[2] Edward Wimberly extends this concept of refugees to those who have cut themselves off from family and past generations. These are "relational refugees" who have severed their ties with community, church, living family members, and ancestors.[3]

A "relational refugee" is depicted by Toni Morrison in her novel *Home*.[4] The protagonist Frank Money joins the army to escape the confines and dangers of life for a black man in the 1950s in Lotus,

---

[1] W.E.B. Du Bois, *The Souls of Black Folk* (New York: Fawcett Premier Book, fourth printing), pp.16-17. The original was published in 1903 by A.C. McClurg & Co. in Chicago.
[2] Archie Smith, Jr, *Navigating the Deep River: Spirituality in African American Families* (Cleveland: United Church Press, 1997), p.36.
[3] Edward P. Wimberly, *Relational Refugees: Alienation and Reincorporation in African American Churches and Communities* (Nashville: Abingdon, 2000), p.22.
[4] Toni Morrison, *Home* (New York, Random House, 2012).

Georgia. He is forced to return to rescue his little sister, Cee. Like a modern Odysseus, he must meet challenges, especially the memories of brutality and violence in the farm country of Georgia. Unlike the bicultural children interviewed for this research, Frank Money had a distinct sense of his identity from childhood to adulthood.

The particularity in my usage of the term "transplanted bicultural child" has to do with the child's immediate and physical engagement/disengagement with the environment. The bodily interaction with the earthly context and the tactile engagement with caretakers not only imprints the consciousness of the developing child, but makes the "transplanting" a sensory shock. "Transplant shock" is a term from plant biology and is used specifically when a living organism with a root system is moved into a different soil environment. Trees must be transplanted with great care. Transplanting can be a danger to the root system if the "root ball" is not protected and transferred intact. After replanting, it takes an average of three years for the root system to rejuvenate.[5]

Borrowing language from plant biology, I have been exploring how a child can be transplanted from one cultural soil to another and avoid transplant shock and stress. How can the "root ball" remain intact? How does a transplanted child maintain its existing growth? How does a child re-root herself socially? What is the optimal climate for roots to rejuvenate?

To be clear on my usage of the term "bicultural child," let me offer the true and painful story of Fauziya from Ghana.[6] Fauziya experienced the clash of two subcultures in Ghana and left Ghana at age 17. In her father's house, she knew she would not be subject to forced marriage, polygamy, or genital mutilation. Her father did not believe in these customs. However, Fauziya's father died when she was 17. She was left in the care of her paternal aunt who did believe in all of the aforementioned customs: arranged marriage, polygamy, genital circumcision. Fauziya was betrothed to a 45-year-old man whom she did not know. She was scheduled for ritual female mutilation and would be one of several wives. She was caught in a subcultural divide. She fled to the USA where she was treated poorly as she waited for refugee status. She was eventually granted refuge from persecution. As Archie Smith delineates this narrative, it is obvious that Fauziya experienced subcultural shock in her homeland and adjustment issues upon immigrating to the USA. She as a refugee is "uprooted" from

---

[5] Jackie Burghardt, Colorado Master Gardener, Colorado State University, Denver, CO. Online article titled "What Happens to a Tree When it is Moved?" http://www.colostate.edu/Depts/CoopExt/4DMG/Trees/movetree.htm.
[6] Op.cit., Smith, pp.36-37.

her home culture in Ghana. However, her early years of identity formation were spent in Ghana; Fauziya would not be a bicultural child as I am using the term. Rather, the terms international or intercultural might suit her emerging identity as a young adult for surely her new life in the USA will impact her identity consolidation as an adult.

Although Fausiya immigrated to the USA with the fresh memory of "cultural trauma" in the form of narrowly-avoided arranged marriage, polygamy, and genital mutilation, others from African countries are contributing to cultural studies with instances of "distant traumatic memories" as conveyed by ancestral lineage. The multigenerational dimension of cultural trauma "resides in its capacity to function as a 'memory performance' that conjures a left-behind homeland in order to help African Americans make meaning out of our traumatic encounters in the United States."[7]

In a "Feelings Release Workshop" in Atlanta, Georgia, in 1992, a participant entered a relaxed state under the expert supervision of trained clinical psychologists. In this relaxed, perhaps regressed state of consciousness, the participant experienced a heaviness on her chest, labored breathing, and constrictions on her wrists and ankles. The two attending therapists crouched by the mat on which she lay. They surmised that what she was experiencing were labor pains; the participant and her husband had just adopted an infant after years of infertility treatments. However, upon regaining awareness of time and space, the patient was adamant: she had experienced the travail of the slave ships. She had felt the shackles on her wrists and ankles and the trauma of being shipped in slavery. Multigenerational transmission of distant cultural trauma is a particular aspect of *cultural consolidation* and identity formation that begs further investigation as the complexities of identity are realized. The generalizability of the cases I have used in this section point to the undeniable conclusion: human developmental theory has not incorporated the intricacies of the bicultural child or the child/adolescent exposed to warring subcultures or the young adult's recall of distant ancestral memories.

---

[7] Cedric C. Johnson, synopsis to his paper, "Globalization, Cultural Trauma and the Reconstruction of Diasporic African Identities," given at the Society for Pastoral Theology's Workshop on Postcolonialism, Globalization, and Pastoral Care Working Group, June 14, 2013, Decatur, Georgia.

Tendrils of Power

Power dynamics lurk in every institution, every structure, including that of missions. As an example, British, Canadian, and American missionaries worked together before World War II in Shandong, China, to build a Christian University: Cheeloo University. Ruth Carson West, daughter of agricultural and educational missionaries, spoke of this venture in Chapter Five. Ruth revealed in a subsequent interview that there were levels of power among the missionaries: The British had the most power, then the Canadians, and last, those from the USA. In other words, there was a pecking order. Although Ruth described the work as "constructive cooperation," there was a ranking of power on the missionary station. Such ecumenical endeavors are always acts of hope in faith and are set against the background of national political receptivity. As a child, Ruth also was increasingly aware of the Chinese national power fluctuations; the missionaries were welcomed because Chiang Kai-shek and Sun Yat-sen were in power. The situation shifted dramatically when Mao Zedong was the dominant player.

In her later interview, Ruth also tells of a time when she was asked to relinquish power. By this time her father was President of Silliman College in the Philippines. Ruth succeeded in receiving the highest grade point average of her graduating class. However, the Filipino Principal called her into his office and informed her that a boy from the Philippines, Wentworth, was going to be valedictorian. Ruth knew she had a higher GPA. When she commented on this, the Principal reminded her of the advantages she had had in her broad and excellent education. He held firm that Wentworth was to be valedictorian. Wentworth was the son of a Chinese plantation owner in the neighboring province. Wentworth, an excellent student, wanted to become a physician and deserved the honor. Ruth accepted this. Many years later, she returned to Philippines and tried to find Wentworth. He had been killed in the war. "What if I had insisted on my way?" A faculty member from Union Theological Seminary in Manila, Philippines, recently told me it was the custom, regardless of gender, that Filipinos would win the awards at Silliman College. This was power relinquished. Ruth also affirmed the values established in promoting Filipino national independence.

It may be that children like Ruth had socio-economic advantages. Perhaps there was cultural superiority in some missionary exchanges. Perhaps there were narcissistic personalities as in all fields. However, the individuals I interviewed are among some of the most egalitarian and self-effacing persons I have known. Many faced ridicule upon return to their homelands and were cast as outsiders. Perhaps this is another reason for their sensitivity to inclusivity. Postcolonial critiques of missions in general will surely recognize that the children born in distant lands had no say as to their situation. In Chapter One, I quoted Edgar, son of missionaries, who gave me an interview while in his late twenties. Now in his late fifties, he is settled in an international community and is married with stepchildren. His faith is still the centering factor in his life; however, he would not now claim to be rootless. I have used the following excerpt from his original interview because it gave me a first glimpse of the phenomenon of *cultural dissolution.*

> [Faith] has given our lives their shape. The fact that our parents are committed to it has determined where we are born, where educated, who our friends are, the fact we fit in no culture. We don't. We are blessed and cursed for the fact that we live on a bridge. I will never be totally American, never totally African. When insecure, which is more common, I don't belong anywhere....I share my parents' commitment now, but I still have no roots. [Edgar]

The tendrils of power can twist and turn. Tendrils are mentioned more in the fields of botany and sociology then they are in the field of politics, religion, and sociology. However, whatever the field, tendrils can ensnare another organism and stunt its growth.

Another way to look at this analysis of power dynamics is through the analysis of *cultural capital.* Cultural capital can mean social assets that produce mobility. The term "cultural capital" as introduced by Pierre Bourdieu and Claude Passeron in 1973 does not include financial assets. There are three subsets of cultural capital: embodied cultural assets, objective capital, and institutional capital. The children of missionaries like Ruth could have experienced the following: *embodied cultural assets* as the whiteness of skin, the blueness of eyes, the silkiness of women's hands, height and sturdy shoulders of men, more options for clothing, better stitched clothing; *objective capital* as a radio, a telephone, a transmitter, a vacation, a TV, a piece of art; *institutional capital* as educational degrees, ability to speak multiple languages, the ability to read, the status of a minister or holy person. These are only a few examples in the three subsets.

Surely these issues occur whenever a child is transplanted. These issues arise when a child is transplanted away from the homeland and also transplanted back into the home culture. *Embodied cultural liabilities* upon return might include the following: awkwardness about "dating," lack of familiarity with games and sports, clothing out of the "mission barrel," lack of familiarity with idioms. *Objective liabilities* could entail: lack of gadgets, use of public transportation, no drivers' education. *Institutional liabilities are many*: unease with the American educational system, lack of peer group, absence of AP courses, unfamiliarity with clubs and social organizations like sororities, Honor Society, and Beta Club.

Ever since Charles Darwin wrote *On the Movements and Habits of Climbing Plants*, botanists have been better informed on varieties of tendrils and on the motion of stems and tendrils.[8] Darwin called the motion: *circumnutation*. This tendency to move or climb as a motion toward support may be an appropriate metaphor for the developing, perhaps transplanted, bicultural child. Tendrils can determine the direction and intensity of growth. However, tendrils of parasitic plants are a cellular invasion. Thus, a study of developmental issues in the transplanted bicultural child would benefit from an awareness of the intricacies of *circumnutation*!

The Deltoid Pumpkin Seed:
The Hybrid Space of Bill Miller

In great secrecy, on a private airstrip about fifty miles southwest of New York, Aereon 7 got ready to fly....The 7, as the aircraft was called, was bright orange. It had no wings. It had a deep belly and a broad, arching back. Seen from above, it was a delta. From the side, it looked like a fat and tremendous pumpkin seed.[9]

So begins John McPhee's chronicle of an experimental aerobody that is not only one man's mission and dream, but his successful attempt to bring two worlds together. This tenacious man is Bill Miller of Princeton, son of missionaries to Iran. Bill's paternal grandfather and great-grandfather were pastors. His maternal grandparents owned Lukens Steel Company. His grandmother supported his parents' Iran mission work and later co-founded InterVarsity Christian Fellowship (IVCF). Bill's family helped lay the foundations of his faith or the "theological substrate," as Bill named it. "The absence of the closeness of the mission field was something I missed here in the USA." Bill respected his father, but he didn't want to be a "carbon copy." Therefore, when asked, "Are you going to be a missionary

---

[8] Charles Darwin, monograph, *On the Movements and Habits of Climbing Plants* (New York: Appleton, 1876, 2nd ed. rev.).

[9] John McPhee, *The Deltoid Pumpkin Seed* (New York: Farrar, Straus and Giroux, 1973), p.3.

[like your father]," he would wisely answer: "I want to be a missionary and a pilot."

Meshed, Iran, was his birthplace, and it was in Meshed that Bill saw his first plane. Although Meshed had no airfield, a small plane took his mother to Teheran to get dental work. Bill waited for his mother to return. In a recent interview, he recalled the azure blue sky and the tiny engine noise. "Here came a solitary airplane…my mother is in that airplane!" As a little boy, he was ecstatic. His impulse was to run to the hills and touch the sky. "That episode was very distinct in my love of flying. My mother was always getting me goggles and [all sorts of things] with wings on them." Bill met resistance from his paternal grandmother who declared if the Lord had wanted us to fly, [the Lord] "would have given us wings." After helping raise him and his sister in Meshed, his grandmother's harrowing flight in a small plane over the Alborz mountains was never forgotten.

Back in the USA, he relished building and flying model airplanes. He attended two schools before the Choate School, where he was allowed to study Aeronautics instead of Latin. Graduating in 1944, he could find no military aircraft design program so he stated: "If I can't design them, maybe I can fly them." Bill felt like a social misfit or outsider back in the States. He experienced bullying in school because he "was from Iran." Bill was bilingual and accustomed to Persian music and European classical music. "There's a loneliness about being a missionary child because so many others don't have the same experience…. [that is] a reservoir of broad-gauged cross-cultural experience that most people lack. It is hard to have discourse with others whose spectrum is less wide. People are less animated by the same range of interests." Bill enlisted in the Navy; he was commissioned a Naval Aviator in 1947. When he earned his navy wings, his mother pinned on his Wings of Gold. He describes this as a "high point" of his life. He served four more years in the Navy as an Attack Pilot on the USS Kearsage in the Atlantic Fleet. He completed a college degree at Princeton University while serving as a Fighter Pilot in the reserves. Bill served with various Christian organizations while also holding on to his dream to design an airplane.

Bill describes himself as "born again" in Ontario at a summer IVCF Leadership camp. This pivotal rebirth was an answer to his parent's prayers; Bill overcame his antipathy to consider missionary service. He enrolled for three years at Biblical Seminary in New York City. IVCF enlisted him to minister in New York City to foreign students; his "home hospitality" program fostered a "home away from home." Over twenty-two churches and 150 families hosted over 300 students. Bill left for a world trip to follow up these students and to engage in a vocational discernment period. After traversing 68 countries in over 20 months, Bill returned to three disappointments: he was not accepted into a Ph.D. program at Princeton Theological Seminary, his empirical, poly-cultural insights were not welcomed by IVCF, and his marriage plans collapsed. Bill described these three rejections as "derailing his quest" and inducing an "emotional instability." During his stop in Iran on his world tour, Bill had become reconciled to serving "in his father's shadow," as the youth worker leader for the Church Council of Iran. However, he became disillusioned with the institutional church, and his desire for service in the church ended.

His discovery of Scripture Union's world ministry to children – an infrastructure for university student work – led him to volunteer in the U.S. His service as a leader of the Children's Sand and Surf Missions brought emotional healing and led to summer missions (1963-2001) which became his real "missionary service."

In 1960, Rev. Monroe Drew, minister of Fourth Presbyterian Church in Trenton, NJ, and a Navy Chaplain, came across the work of a Civil War inventor, Solomon Andrews, who "built and flew a triple-hulled, gravity-powered airship he called the AEREON."[10] Drew envisioned a large, hybrid airship (part airship and part airplane) to haul supplies to missionaries in far flung places. This would develop into the Faith Fleet! "His dreams were grandiose – an enormous Faith Fleet that would serve Christian missions by carrying huge cargoes swiftly and cheaply to the underdeveloped countries that needed the goods as well as the Gospel. He tried to involve the Presbyterian Church deeply in the venture."[11] Bill Miller inadvertently saw a photo of the hybrid aircraft on the desk of his stockbroker one day and was immediately enthralled. Here was a way to consolidate his love of missions and his passion for flying. He quickly realized a "Faith Fleet" distributing Bibles had little economic promise, but he saw the rare opportunity to help create something truly new in aviation with potential profits to support Christian missions. Like the hybridity of the airship, his future work with AEREON would be the hybrid of his two callings. Bill joined the board of directors and eventually became President and CEO of AEREON. Today, at 88, with most of his life savings invested in the corporation, Bill works to get a second generation hybrid off the ground despite the company's inability to secure

[10] Lane Wallace, "Flying Lessons," in *Flying: The World's Most Widely Read Aviation Magazine*, June 2010, pp. 92-93.
[11] Edmund Fuller, "Getting A Dream Off the Ground," *The Wall Street Journal*. September 5, 1973.

sustainable support. Although Bill's pioneer hybrid technology has not yet won institutional traction, he has been awarded three US aircraft patents.

In concluding the interview, Bill remembered his austere father telling him as a young adult that his continuing love of aviation was childish. He also recalled the words of the deputy for Vice Admiral Cebrowski in the Department of Defense telling him in 2003, "Bill, you were 30 years ahead of your time."

On one of many test runs of the aerobody, John McPhee described Bill Miller in his Navy flight jacket, issued 25 years earlier. "His past seemed somewhat at odds with his theological present – the Master of Theology whose time-and-a-half labors for AEREON were virtually equaled by his continuing church work...."[12] Then McPhee pays him a great compliment and effectively describes *cultural consolidation*: "Miller, however, had long since reconciled the divergences in his cosmology...."[13]

The Burlap Sack

> I have learned for so many years to live with my roots packed in soil, and each place that I go, I brush a little of the soil of the place over the roots, but I never unpack them. [It is like they are wrapped in a burlap sack, penetrable to water.] You just brush a little bit of the soil of the place over it so you're as inconspicuous as possible. (Edgar, missionary son, after his return to the USA from Ghana).

A burlap sack is often used in transplanting. Of course, the consistency of the burlap, the coverage of roots[14] and wire or cord around the burlap are differentials. Burlap made of natural fiber allows for more oxygen to reach the roots, and it disintegrates faster. Treated and synthetic burlap can hinder the spreading of the roots as they adapt. Gentle treatment of the living organism is always expected lest the root ball be damaged. It is recommended that no more than 2/3 of the root system be left in burlap when transplanted; otherwise, adaptation is hindered. If the burlap is secured with wire, and the wire is not removed, the root system will not develop fully.

I mention the wrapping of the roots in detail to highlight the variables. Numerous variables will be present in life stories of bicultural children who experience a re-rooting. It is important for those stories to be told. This book is an encouragement for all the individual narratives.

---

[12] McPhee, op.cit., p.76.

[13] Ibid., p.77.

[14] It is recommended that two-thirds of the root system be covered.

The history of a root system that always remains in its native soil will be different from a transplanted system. So it is with children. Developmental theories that do not take this into account will be as constrictive of healthy developmental adaptation as the wire binding burlap.

How does a child move with the root ball intact? How is one handled gently in the transplanting? The following account of a successful re-rooting is given by Samuel Moffett, 97 years of age. He comments from the vantage point of a fruitful and abundant life.

Samuel Moffett: The Fabric of Korean Life

Samuel Hugh Moffett is the son of distinguished missionaries to Korea. Dr. Moffett was born in Pyengyang, Korea, in 1916. He came to the USA to complete a ministerial degree at Princeton Theological Seminary followed by a doctorate at Yale University. He subsequently went to China as a missionary from 1947-1951 until he was detained and expelled by the Chinese communists. He then became a missionary in Korea where he served until 1981 in theological education. In 1981, Dr. Moffett became Professor of Mission and Ecumenics at Princeton Theological Seminary and was named professor emeritus when he retired in 1986. He has authored numerous works, among them, *A History of Christianity in Asia.* In the introduction of *Scenes from the Hermit Kingdom*, Dr. Moffett states: "Our family has been immersed in the fabric of Korean life for most of the twentieth century, beginning with the final decade of the 19th."[15]

The burlap sack for Dr. Samuel Moffett was, in part, the fabric of Korean life. I had two occasions to witness this. First, in my sabbatical residency in Princeton, I noticed the steady stream of Korean students who came to meet him because of their family connections with him. At one meal that I shared with Samuel and Eileen Moffett, a niece of one of his former Korean translators was part of the extended family. Secondly, in interviewing and videotaping Samuel Moffett, he disclosed that he did not thrive after he was born in 1916 in Korea. A missionary friend recommended a Korean "milk mother," and Samuel was nursed at her breast for months. When asked where he felt at home, he said: "I am Korean. I have Korean blood in my veins." I showed this portion of the tape at a Korean-Global Mission Leadership Forum in New Haven, CT.

---

[15] Samuel Hugh Moffett, introduction to *Scenes from the Hermit Kingdom: Selected Photographs from the Moffett Korea Collection*, ed. Sarah Malone and PTS Library Staff (Princeton: SCPTS Monograph, 2007).

There were 25 delegates from Korea, 25 from the USA. The admiration for Dr. Moffett among the Korean delegates was evident. The pride among the Korean contingent when he claimed kinship was palpable. In the taped interview, Dr. Moffett concedes that he is at home in both cultures: the USA and Korea. However, the fabric of Korean life was somehow part of that which contained and protected his roots in moving.

Dr. Moffett did honestly convey the difficulties of re-rooting in the USA upon return for college. He attended Wheaton College which provided fertile soil for his faith. His ability to play soccer was a means of adapting to the environment. He was an excellent student and gifted in language study. Nevertheless, the storms of sadness swept over him as he entered Princeton Seminary. On his second day of seminary, he received word that his beloved father, Samuel A. Moffett, had died. It was the understanding and guidance of the seminary president, Dr. Mackay, that helped him through this great loss. Dr. Mackay and Jane Logan Wells Mackay were former missionaries. Members of the family of faith like the Mackays surrounded Samuel in Princeton. Communities of support like this often serve as "a burlap sack." To borrow a psychological term, family, ancestors, cultural beliefs, and one's faith can function as a *container* for that which is in flux.

"I remember roses": The Lost Generation

In the basement level of The Art Gallery of New South Wales, a startling exhibit of Brenda Croft's color ilfachrome photographs titled "In My Father's House" reveal the pain of the dislocation of what is now being called "the lost generation" of Australia. Her father, Joseph Croft, like many aboriginal children in the 1920s in Australia, was stolen from family and put in a children's home [Kahlin Compound] in Darwin. He was moved to a variety of places like the Half-caste Children's Home in Alice Springs. In 1974, as a middle-aged man applying for a birth certificate, he was told by the Northern Territory Government that his mother was still alive! His daughter, aboriginal artist Brenda Croft, tells his story and that of other Australian children in her photography.

In 1905, the Aborigines Act in Australia legalized the removal of small children from Aboriginal families. The aim was to turn lighter-skinned Aboriginal children into "white" citizens. These children were placed in homes to be adopted by white families. Only in 1967, by Referendum, did Aboriginals become Australian citizens.

"I remember roses" is one Croft photograph from her series titled"In My Father's House," that impresses the viewer with the strength of a stolen child's early sensory imprints. It is a collage of fragmentation. In the center and dominating the collage is a white family with an adopted aboriginal child, a boy. The center photo was taken in a lovely garden with roses cascading over a wall. In the lower left corner of the collage, is the aboriginal mother holding the same boy as an infant – again surrounded by wild roses in an earlier garden. A photo of the child peers out from the top of the collage. "I remember roses…." Are these the roses of both gardens? It is perhaps Brenda Croft's father, remembering his transplantation from one garden to another by way of sensory memories!

Brenda Croft fills the whole room with images of displaced and transplanted children. She says of the tragic images:

> 'In My Father's House' is a memorial not only to my father and brother but a memorial to all those children stolen from their families and denied knowledge of their heritage. This work is about chasing and catching those memories as they fall.[16]

"Don't go kissing at the garden gate" is a memory of a small girl being taken from her aboriginal parents as the long line of her siblings stand behind the biological mother. The new white mother is beaming in contrast to the doleful expression of the aboriginal mother who stares sternly forward and away from the severing of her family. The garden gate is the scene of abandonment.

In an adjacent room at the Sydney museum are video installations by Genevieve Grieves, Worimi artist in Sydney, Australia.[17] In "Picturing the Old People" [2005], one video installation titled "Family" shows an aboriginal child being silently removed from a sibling grouping. One small child simply vanishes from the family grouping so subtly that the viewer is almost unaware – almost.

The work of Brenda Croft and Genevieve Grieves an artists and my research as a theologian converge. The constructed layers of memory in Croft's work reflect the fragmented lives of these children and the ongoing effects of this through generations as families reconnect. "In this process memories become distorted and disparate elements inform one's sense of self, while questioning the validity of one's thoughts."[18] My research shows that transplanting the bicultural child can result in fragmentation of one's cultural identity and sense of self. This creates a more arduous

---

[16] Brenda Croft, script on wall plaque dated 1998, The Art Museum of New South Wales, Sydney, Australia.
[17] Half Light Portraits from Black Australia, op. cit., pp.76-81.
[18] Museum commentary, plaque on wall.

journey towards *cultural consolidation*. It can be done as many of the
narratives of courageous bicultural children have shown. Successful
transplanting can result in a stronger, more resilient, gifted, creative self.
Some people do not make it. Some transplanted lives still tackle the
odyssey of consolidation, of finding home, of putting down roots. Violet
Bacon, a Yamatji woman facing her aboriginal history concluded:

> What is this thing that people call identity? What does it mean? It was a
> long time before I understood what it was for me. A feeling of togetherness
> with my spirit, an essence of spirituality, of Dreaming that needs to be
> nourished so it will grow strong and tall. The tree of identity, that's how I
> think of it. I picture a tall towering gum tree with strong branches, a solid
> trunk and no leaves. Why no leaves? Because then I can see clearly.[19]

Tjalaminu Mia, a Nyungar woman in Australia, was placed as a child
into Sister Kate's Children's Home. While there she noted "something
very deep was missing in my life and it was that deep sense of being
connected to my people, my family, my ancestors and to our cultural
beliefs. It was a spirituality that Sunday School teachers couldn't
understand and because of this oppression I started to lose my sense of
being a Nyungar kid."[20] She was able to find her "taproot," that is,in her
words, the root of the tree that goes the deepest. The taproot for her was
the foundation of connection to the spiritual realm of her culture. Identity
consolidation can be achieved with an adequate holding environment. A
taproot is one such example.

There will be many types of bicultural children. The varieties of
portable roots will be as numerous as will be the forms of "burlap sacks"
of cultural intimacy. What this research has attempted to show is the
following: roots are portable; transplanting roots is a complex process that
impacts identity formation. As the work of developmentalists,
psychologists, and psychiatrists incorporates these findings, bicultural
children will cease to be "the lost children" in mainstream developmental
theory. Theologians like myself will be challenged to rethink *diaspora* in
terms of the "rootlessness" unearthed through these narratives of children.
Their courageous delving and digging into their stories can only add to the
fecundity of the soil of our joint scholarship.

---

[19] Violet Bacon, "Joining My Identity Pieces Together, in *Speaking From the Heart: Stories of Life, Family, and Country*, eds.Sally Morgan, Tjalaminu Mia, Blaze Kwaymullina (Fremantle: Fremantle Press, 2009), p.160.
[20] Tjalaminu Mia, "Boorn – Taproot," ibid., p.213.

BIBLIOGRAPHY

A Promised Land, A Perilous Journey: Theological Perspectives on Migrations. Edited by Daniel G. Groody and Gioacchino Campese. Notre Dame: University of Notre Dame, 2008.

Bhabha, Homi K. *The Location of Culture.* New York: Routledge, 1994.

Boughter, C. Luke. "The Family as a Missionary Unit." Thesis, The Graduate School of Missions at Columbia (South Carolina), 1950.

Buck, Pearl S. *The Exile.* New York: John Day, 1936.

—. *A House Divided.* New York: John Day, 1935.

—. *Kinfolk.* New York: John Day, 1948.

—. *My Several Worlds: A Personal Record.* New York: John Day, 1954.

—. *The Child Who Never Grew.* Vineland, New Jersey: The Training School, 1950.

—. *The Living Reed.* New York: John Day, 1963.

Burghardt, Jackie. "What Happens to a Tree When It Is Moved." Colorado State University. http://www.colostate.edu/Depts/CoopExt/4DMG/Trees /movetree.htm.

Danielson, Edward E. *Missionary Kid, MK.* Pasadena, CA: W. Carey Library, 1984.

Darwin, Charles. *On the Movements and Habits of Climbing Plants.* 2nd. Rev. ed. New York: Appleton, 1876.

DeGracia, Donna Sidwell. *An Intricate Tapestry: The Acculturation of Missionaries and Their Children.* Minneapolis, MN: Kirk House, 2011.

Diaz, R. "The Intellectual Power of Bilingualism." *Journal of the American Academy of Child and Adolescent Psychiatry* 38 (September 1999): 1197.

Downie, Richard. "Re-entry Experience and Identity Formation of Third Culture Experienced Dependent American Youth: An Exploratory Study." Thesis, Michigan State University, 1976.

Downs, Ray. "A Look at the Third Culture Child." *Japan Christian Quarterly* 42, no. 2 (Spring 1976).

Du Bois, W. E. B. *The Souls of Black Folk.* Greenwich, CT: Fawcett Publications, 1961.

Dungan, David L. *A History of the Synoptic Problem: The Canon, the Text, the Composition, and the Interpretation of the Gospels.* New York: Doubleday, 1999.

Erikson, Erik H. *Childhood and Society*. 2nd ed. New York: W. W. Norton, 1963.

—. *Identity: Youth, and Crisis*. New York: W. W. Norton, 1968.

Family Accountability In Missions: Korean and Western Case Studies. Edited by Jonathan J. Bonk. New Haven: OMSC Publications, 2013.

Farley, Wendy. *Gathering Those Driven Away: A Theology of Incarnation*. Louisville: Westminster John Knox Press, 2011.

Freud, Sigmund. *Character and Culture*. New York: Macmillam, 1963.

Fu, Ping, and MeiMei Fox. *Bend, Not Break: A Life in Two Worlds*. New York: Portfolio/Penguin, 2012.

Fuller, Edmund. "Getting A Dream Off the Ground." *The Wall Street Journal*, September 5, 1973.

Gray, Charlene J. *Children of the Call: Issues Missionaries' Kids Face*. Birmingham, Ala.: New Hope, 1995.

Half and Half: Writers on Growing Up Biracial and Bicultural. Edited by Claudine Chiawei O'Hearn. New York: Pantheon, 1998.

Hersey, John Richard. *A Bell for Adano*. New York: A. Knopf, 1944.

—. *Hiroshima*. New York: Random House, 1946.

—. *White Lotus*. New York: Alfred A. Knopf, 1965.

Hesse, Hermann. *Briefe: Erweiterte Ausgabe*. Frankfurt Am Main: Suhrkamp Verlag, 1964.

—. *Peter Camenzind*. Translated by Michael Roloff. New York: Farrar, Straus and Giroux, 1969.

Holmes, Barbara Ann. *Race and the Cosmos: An Invitation to View the World Differently*. Harrisburg, PA: Trinity Press International, 2002.

Holton, M. Jan. *Building the Resilient Community: Lessons from the Lost Boys of Sudan*. Eugene, Oregon: Cascade, 2011.

Iyer, Pico. *The Global Soul: Jet Lag, Shopping Malls, and the Search for Home*. New York: Vintage, 2000.

Jessup, Henry Harris. *Fifty-three Years in Syria*. Vol. I and II. New York: Fleming H. Revell, 1910.

Johnson, Cedric C. "Globalization, Cultural Trauma and the Reconstruction of Diasporic African Identities." Society for Pastoral Theology's Workshop on Postcolonialism, Globalization, and Pastoral Care Working Group, Decatur, Georgia, June 14, 2013.

Jung, Carl Gustav. *Erinnerungen, Träume, Gedanken*. Zürich: Rascher, 1963.

Jung, Shannon, Jeanne Hoeft, and Joretta Marshall. *Practicing Care in Rural Congregations and Communities*. Minneapolis: Fortress Press, 2013.

Kluckhohn, Clyde. *Mirror For Man: The Relation of Anthropology to Modern Life*. New York: Whittlesey House, 1949.

Kluger, Jeffrey. "The Power of the Bilingual Brain." *Time* 182, no. 5 (2013): 42-47.

Larson, Linnea Carol. "A Program of Guidance in the Missionary Boarding School Based on Self-Concept System." Thesis, Kansas State University, 1971.

Law, Eric H. F. *The Word at the Crossings: Living the Good News in a Multicontextual Community*. St. Louis: Chalice, 2004.

Lee, Jung Young. *Marginality: The Key to Multicultural Theology*. Minneapolis: Fortress, 1995.

Levine, Donald. "Simmel at a Distance: On the History and the Systematics of the Sociology of the Stranger." *Sociological Focus* 10, no. 1 (January 1997): 15-29.

Levitt, Peggy. *God Needs No Passport: Immigrants and the Changing American Religious Landscape*. New York: The New Press, 2007.

Lorch, Hilde. *Wolken, Winde Und Sonnenschein*. Stuttgart: Evang. Missionsverlag, 1936.

Marrer-Tising, Carlee. *The Reception of Hermann Hesse by the Youth in the U.S.: A Thematic Analysis*. Bern: Peter Lang Verlag, 1982.

McPhee, John. *The Deltoid Pumpkin Seed*. New York: Farrar, Straus and Giroux, 1973.

Mead, Margaret, and Franz Boas. *Coming of Age in Samoa: A Psychological Study of Primitive Youth for Western Civilization*. New York: Morrow, 1928.

Moffett, Samuel H. *Scenes from the Hermit Kingdom: Selected Photographs from the Moffett Korea Collection*. Edited by Sarah A. Malone, Eileen F. Moffett, Clifford B. Anderson, and Stephen D. Crocco. Princeton, NJ: Princeton Theological Seminary, 2007.

Morrison, Toni. *Home*. New York: Random House, 2012.

Niebuhr, H. Richard. *Christ and Culture*. New York: Harper & Row, 1951.

Peña, Manuel H. *Where the Ox Does Not Plow: A Mexican American Ballad*. Albuquerque: University of New Mexico Press, 2008.

Perkins, Hetti, and Jonathan Jones. *Half Light: Portraits from Black Australia*. Sydney, NSW: Art Gallery of New South Wales, 2008.

Phan, Peter C. *Christianity With an Asian Face*. Maryknoll: Orbis Books, 2003.

Reddy, Sumathi. "Wise Beyond Their Years: What Babies Really Know." *Wall Street Journal*, February 12, 2013.

Rice, Noodles, Bread or Chapati. Edited by Polly C. Ho. Singapore: Third Culture Kids Care Fellowship, 2013.

Rieger, Joerg, and Kwok Pui-lan. *Occupy Religion: Theology of the Multitude.* Lanham, Maryland: Rowman & Littlefield Publishers, 2012.

Rieger, Joerg. *Traveling: Christian Explorations of Daily Living.* Minneapolis: Fortress, 2011.

Roberts, Michelle Voss. *Dualities: A Theology of Difference.* Louisville: Westminster John Knox Press, 2010.

Ryle, Gilbert. "The Thinking of Thoughts: What Is 'Le Penseur' Doing?" Lecture, University of Saskatchewan, 1968. In *Collected Papers.* Vol. II. Hutchison, 1971.

Schnieper, Werner. "Baslerstab Kolumne." *Baslerstab*, July 31, 1982.

Servín, Manuel P. *The Mexican-Americans: An Awakening Minority.* Beverly Hills: Glencoe Press, 1970.

Shifron, Rachel. "Adler's Need to Belong as the Key for Mental Health." *The Journal of Individual Psychology* 66, no. 1 (Spring 2010): 10-29.

Simmel, Georg. *Soziologie.* Leipzig: Duncker & Humblot, 1908.

Smith, Archie, Jr. *Navigating the Deep River: Spirituality in African American Families.* Cleveland, OH: United Church Press, 1997.

Speaking From the Heart: Stories of Life, Family, and Country. Edited by Sally Morgan, Tjalaminu Mia, and Blaze Kwaymullina. Fremantle: Fremantle Arts Centre Press, 2007.

Stevenson-Moessner, Jeanne. *In Her Own Time: Women and Developmental Issues in Pastoral Care.* Minneapolis: Fortress Press, 2000.

—. "Alien at Home: The Point of Entry." in *Family Accountability In Missions: Korean and Western Case Studies.* Edited by Jonathan J. Bonk. New Haven: OMSC Publications, 2013: 59-69.

—. "Cultural Dissolution: 'I Lost Africa.'" in *Missiology: An International Review.* Vol. XIV. No. 3. Scottdale, Penn.: American Society of Missiology, 1986.

—. *Theological Dimensions of Maturation in a Missionary Milieu.* Berne: P. Lang, 1989.

Tanner, Kathryn. *Theories of Culture: A New Agenda for Theology.* Minneapolis: Fortress Press, 1997.

Turkle, Sherry. *Alone Together: Why We Expect More from Technology and Less from Each Other.* New York: Basic Books, 2011.

Unrooted Childhoods: Memoirs of Growing Up Global. Edited by Faith Eidse and Nina Sichel. London: Nicholas Brealey Publishing, 2004.

Useem, Ruth Hill. "The American Family in India." *The Annals of the American Academy of Political and Social Science* 368 (November 1966): 132-45.

Useem, Ruth Hill, and Richard Dixon Downie. "Third Culture Kids." *Today's Education*, September/October 1976, 103-05.

Von Schiller, Johann Christoph Friedrich. *William Tell Schauspiel.* Tuebingen: Cotta, 1804.

Wallace, Lane. "Flying Lessons." *Flying: The World's Most Widely Read Aviation Magazine*, June 2010.

Weil, Simone. *The Need for Roots*. London: Routledge & Paul, 1952.

Welch, William, and Marisol Bello. "A Perfect Recipe for a Predator." *USA Today*, February 10, 2012.

Wilson, Colin. *The Outsider*. London: V. Gollanz, 1956.

Wimberly, Edward P. *Relational Refugees: Alienation and Reincorporation in African American Churches and Communities.* Nashville: Abingdon Press, 2000.

Wong, Patricia C. M., Alice H. D. Chan, Anil Roy, and Elizabeth Hellmuth Margulis. "The Bimusical Brain Is Not Two Monomusical Brains in One: Evidence from Musical Affective Processing." *Journal of Cognitive Neuroscience* 23, no. 12 (2011): 4082-93.

Writing out of Limbo: International Childhoods, Global Nomads and Third Culture Kids. Edited by Gene H. Bell-Villada, Nina Sichel, Faith Eidse and Elaine Neil Orr. Newcastle upon Tyne, UK: Cambridge Scholars Pub., 2011.

INDEX

A

The Aborigines Act of Australia, 102
AEREON, 99, 100
Adler, Alfred, 68
American University of Beirut, 83, 84
The Art Gallery of New South Wales, 102
Au pair, 58

B

Bacon, Violet, 104
Balmer, Randall, xiii
Banks, Andy, xvii
Basel Mission Children's Home, xviii, 8, 67
Bell-Villada, Gene, 26, 29
Bialac, Verda Hostetler, xv
bicultural child, 2, 6, 7, 8, 10, 12, 13, 21, 24, 33, 34, 78, 80, 88, 91, 92, 93, 94, 97, 103
bilingualism, 12
bimusical mind, 12, 13
Black Forest Academy, xvii, xix, 7, 8, 39, 52
bonding, 45, 46, 47, 52, 53, 54, 58, 61, 68
Boughter, C. Luke, 40
Boxer Uprising, 3
Brush, Stanley Elwood, xiv
Buck, Pearl S, 2, 3, 5, 15, 39, 69, 73, 76, 77, 78, 80
The Burlap Sack, 100

C

CARLA, 6
Catalyst, 61
Center of Theological Inquiry, xv, xviii, 69
Cetana Education Foundation, 36, 37
Cheeloo University, 32, 70, 95
Coalter, Milton, xiii
consciousness, 10, 13, 29, 93, 94
Cooper-White, Pamela, 9
Croft, Brenda, 102, 103
cultural capital, 96
cultural consolidation, 6, 7, 12, 19, 20, 33, 69, 78, 91, 94, 100, 104
cultural dissolution, 10, 12, 17, 20, 96
cultural enclosure, 39
cultural fragmentation, 19, 30, 31
Cultural intimacy, 3, 10, 11, 33, 76, 104
culture, 6

D

Danielson, Edward E, 40
Darwin, Charles, 97
Davis, Mary McClintock, xviii, 69, 73
DeGracia, Donna Sidwell, 2, 20, 23
The Deltoid Pumpkin Seed, 97
Democratic Republic of Congo, 5, 67
diaspora, 69, 104
die Kameradschaft, 58
double consciousness, 92
double helix, 9
double worlds, 2, 76